Rosemary Butcher: Choreography, Collisions and Collaborations

edited by Rosemary Butcher and Susan Melrose

THE RETURN 2005
Dancer: EUN-HI KIM, Film: MARTIN OTTER

Collisions
ations

TOUCH THE EARTH 1987

previous page STILL-SLOW-DIVIDED 2002

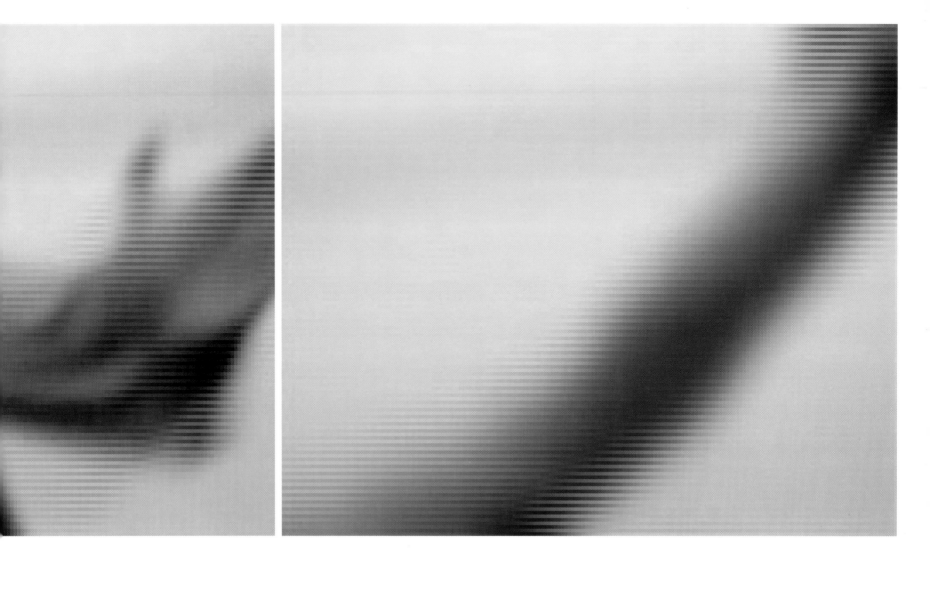

CONTRIBUTING PHOTOGRAPHERS

Pete Anderson
Nicola Baldwin
Gyula Fodor
Nick Georghiou
Hugh Glendenning
Cathy Greenhalgh
Sigune Hamann
Chris Ha (Chris Harris)
Marc Hoflack
David Jackson
Benedict Johnson
Jonathan Keenan
Franz Kimmel
Mark Lewis
Lewis Mulatero
Chris Nash
Martin Otter
Dieter Pietsch
Howard Sooley
Chris Swartz
Geoff White

First published in 2005 by Middlesex University Press

Copyright © Middlesex University Press

ISBN 1904750 47 8

A CIP catalogue for this book is available from The British Library.

Book design by why not associates

Printed in the UK by Cambridge Printing.

Middlesex University Press, Queensway, Enfield, Middlesex EN3 4SA
Tel: +44 (0) 20 8411 5734
Fax: +44 (0) 20 8411 5736
www.mupress.co.uk

Arts & Humanities Research Council

Supported by the Arts and Humanities Research Board through the AHRC's Fellowships in the Creative and Performing Arts scheme.

Tension and Compression
BODY AS SITE 1993, Artist: John Lyall

FOREWORD

IAN BRAMLEY

Choreography, Collisions and Collaborations celebrates the remarkable artistic output of Rosemary Butcher, one of the UK's most original and influential dance artists. For thirty years Butcher has produced challenging, innovative choreography that has stretched the boundaries of the dance art form, applying a rigorous artistic vision to the deployment of bodies in time and space. Butcher has maintained the integrity of this vision from her early experiences in New York's postmodern dance scene at the beginning of the 1970s to the present day through hypnotic minimalist pieces, striking cross art-form collaborations and haunting film works, continually re-inventing the content and re-defining the parameters of her work.

By persistently challenging herself, her collaborators and the viewers of her work, Butcher has established herself as one of the most important choreographers of her generation – maintaining her position at the front-line of the development of dance. But the problem of remaining consistently at the cutting edge means that the audience numbers, sustained funding and consistent critical reception awarded to those who have succumbed to the mainstream remain elusive. If household name status has evaded Butcher, however, there has been a constant recognition of her contribution to the art form. In *Striding Out*, Stephanie Jordan lists Butcher as one of the significant practitioners of new dance in the 1970s and 1980s, the period during which contemporary dance first established itself in the public consciousness in the UK. At the very end of the twentieth century, Butcher found herself included alongside such diverse company as Merce Cunningham and Pina

Bausch in *Fifty Contemporary Choreographers*, which collected entries on key contemporary dance artists from across the globe. There have been two major retrospectives of her work – in 1986 and 1997 – something more usually found in the visual arts than in dance.

Butcher has not, however, been content to remain solely as part of a historic pantheon. In 2004, she entered The Place Prize in order to pit her own creative processes against a new generation of artists and to test the currency and contemporary value of her work. Butcher's entry – *Hidden Voices*, a short, demanding, evocative solo performed by her then-muse Elena Giannotti – reached the final shortlist of five. The critic Ismene Brown lauded it as 'the only genuine piece of art there' and 'a brave, unorthodox, completely imagined miniature worthy of [the prize]… in fact, worthy of the Turner Prize'. It is, of course, the courageousness and maverick nature of Butcher's conceptual choreography that makes her work so interesting and so important.

Brown's quote also highlights the conceptual core of Butcher's work which allows it to stand alongside the visual and other arts. Butcher herself has often felt limited by the definition of her work as choreography and sees herself primarily as an artist whose medium happens to be the human body. This boundary-less approach has facilitated her many collaborations with composers, architects and artists – including Michael Nyman, Zaha Hadid and Turner-prize nominee Vong Phaophanit – and has fuelled her engagement with non-theatrical sites for her work – galleries, the open air, film. Beyond the work itself, Butcher's influence has been widely felt within the dance world through those who have worked with her in the past and through her teaching in the field of higher education. Butcher's dancers are collaborators in the movement she creates and she has attracted the input of some of the most respected contemporary dance interpreters in the UK. A number of her dancers have gone on to become leading choreographers in their own right – amongst them, Jonathan Burrows, Russell Maliphant and Fin Walker. Alongside her career as a creative artist, Butcher has taught choreography at undergraduate and graduate level at vocational colleges and within university departments – including Laban, the University of Surrey and Middlesex University. A demanding yet supportive teacher, who encourages rigour of thought rather than recommending a particular process or aesthetic, Butcher's hidden influence on generations of dance artists has been profound.

This book is a long overdue consideration of Rosemary Butcher's oeuvre with each author bringing a different viewpoint and fresh understanding to her work. As important as the words are the images which accompany them. Despite having created superlative dance-film works, the humanism and understanding of space that Butcher brings to her live works often fails to come across fully in video documentation, but it stands out beautifully in the still images presented here. The combination of the visual and textual provides a unique insight into the work of an extraordinary artist.

Endnotes

1. Jordan, S. *Striding out: Aspects of Contemporary and New Dance in Britain*, London: Dance Books, 1992

2. Sayers, L.-A. 'Rosemary Butcher', *Fifty contemporary choreographers*, M. Bremser (ed.), New York: Routledge, 1999, pp.51-55

3. Brown, I. 'Competition hijacked by the formulaic and banal', *The Daily Telegraph*, 27 September, 2004. Accessed online, 29 June 2005 at: www.telegraph.co.uk/arts/main/jhtml?xml=/arts/2004/09/27/btib27.xml&sSheet/arts/2004/09/27/ixartright.html

BODY AS SITE, IMAGE AS EVENT
Artist: Paul Elliman, 1983

below ROSEMARY BUTCHER IN GROUP
Union Square, New York, 1970
Choreographer: Elaine Summers

ACKNOWLEDGEMENTS

Without the contribution – and the patience – of a number of individuals and funding bodies, this book would quite simply not exist. We want to thank some of them here. First, our thanks to Middlesex University Press, and in particular to Celia Cozens, who took up the project at a very late stage, and has worked so hard on its realisation. Second, our thanks to the Wingate Foundation, for the initial funding which launched the project, and to Ian Bramley, who commissioned most of the essays, and who continued to believe in the project. The design elements are absolutely key to this history of a choreographer and visual artist's work, and we thank the designers, Why Not Associates, and in particular David Ellis, who took on the design challenge of marrying essays and dozens of photographs. (In the case of the photographic images, we have, wherever possible, acknowledged the photographers involved, although some could not be traced. We would ask anyone whose photographic work has not been acknowledged to contact Celia Cozens at the Press.) The writers whose essays are collected here have been remarkably patient and supportive of the project, and we want to thank each of them. Our thanks too to the School of Arts, at Middlesex University, and to the Arts and Humanities Research Council for their commitment to the research programme more generally. Finally, our thanks to Nigel Butcher, to whom the book is dedicated, for his unstinting support.

Susan Melrose & Rosemary Butcher

CONTENTS

AFTER THE CRYING AND THE SHOUTING 1989

INTRODUCTION: OTHER VOICES

SUSAN MELROSE

The different writers included here, who come from a number of professional fields, bring together a range of different approaches to, and engagements with, Rosemary Butcher's work. All have written about that work since the year 2000, and in each case the writing itself can be situated in historical terms (because the work goes on changing). Most of the essays or interviews included are concerned with the relationships between spectating and interpreting aspects of Butcher's work. Most write from the position I myself take up, which is that of the expert spectator-writer. In one case, in place of that spectator-observation, the writer concerned has had access to the performance-*making* processes and to rehearsal. In other cases, the writer has been able to interview the artist herself, thereby supplementing her or his own perceptions of the work. Overall, these different accounts allow us to begin to obtain a composite picture of an artist still at work, still changing, still challenging the British art scene. Despite the insight obtained, however, it seems to me that the sense of mystery or difficulty, which the works have retained over three decades, remains in place.

Four of the writers included here write about *SCAN*, providing overall a fragmented glimpse of the piece in its relationship to spectating and to insider observation. *SCAN* is the major focus of Susan Leigh Foster's essay, and the piece preoccupies Niki Pollard, who has observed its development in rehearsal as well as in public spaces. In Susan Leigh Foster's piece, the writer attempts to provide a 'thick' account of that single work, from the perspective of the expert dancer-spectator and academic writer. She herself weaves together, on the work's behalf, a number of thematic and compositional strands, including action description. Her essay attempts in this way to account for the complexity and 'thickness' of the work itself, what she calls its 'steady urgency', its 'exacting span... precise effort... complete investment'.

The widely published dance critic, Nadine Meisner, takes up and develops the account of a number of key works which are not written about in detail in other essays. She notes a point similar to one made by Hugh Stoddart in the present collection:

Like many artists, Butcher swings between approaches, so that even while her work shows a general trend forward there are still occasional reversions to previous modes and a desire, after exploring one mode, to find relief in another. The movement of other systems-influenced pieces like *Flying Lines* (1985) and the *d1*, *d2* and *3D* trilogy (1989-1990) bisected space in the same way.

Meisner is an astute cultural observer, able to identify both the source of some of Butcher's ideas, and the means by which Butcher proceeds to make them her own: by the time she made *The Site* and *Imprints*, Meisner notes, Butcher 'was creating her movement through the dancers' improvisations, prompted by precise instructions or tasks'. On that basis, which takes up the notion of what I call a 'disciplined-unknowing' in the professional artist (I return to this notion in the final essay in this collection), Meisner observes that Butcher, in the performance-making context, 'sees what the dancers offer her, [but] if the result isn't what she wants, she will refine or change her instruction, but not actually demonstrate what she wants'. Her rule is that the material to which she will put her signature 'has to originate in what the dancers come up with'. 'Like Pina Bausch', Meisner adds, choosing a comparison which is telling, Butcher 'draws up the grand plan, channels the dancers' improvisations, and applies her editorial eye to sift and structure the resulting material'.

Robert Ayers, in formal conversation with Rosemary Butcher, writes from the rather different perspective of a visual arts practitioner, arts writer and academic. In a brief piece which serves principally to introduce the matter of professional collaborations between practising artists, he provides a glimpse of *SCAN* in passing, describing the collaboration central to it as 'a collision' – apparently not atypical – 'between two artistic intelligences': Butcher's own and that of visual artist, Vong Phaophanit. Such collaborations, Butcher notes in turn, tend in her experience to be unequal collisions – providing her, perhaps, with a vehicle which helps her to elaborate the work to which she puts her signature, while enabling the other artist or artists involved to discover a new creative inspiration. Robert Ayers concludes that Butcher's work is 'first cousin to the visual arts', which for their generation are 'allusive, suggestive, to do with real, physical things'.

Niki Pollard, who has observed Rosemary Butcher at work from a privileged 'insider' position over the past decade, takes us into different (rehearsal) spaces from which to view four pieces, *SCAN* (2000), *Three Views from Vertical* (2001)*, Undercurrents* (2001) *and Still-Slow-Divided* (2002)*, in the making. Being present at the making tends, reasonably enough, to reveal aspects of a practitioner's work processes which spectators rarely glimpse. This is in part because processes vital to the making are transformed, in production, and can no longer be seen *as such*. The often vital impact of contingency and happy (or unhappy) accident, as well as the vital 'expert-intuitive' processes of the different performers or collaborators involved, are lost as such. Instead, spectators tend to see what has emerged when production decisions are brought to bear on, and effectively re-order, the more fragile emergent aspects of choreographic, dancerly, or visual arts invention.

   Focusing on the arts practices which Rosemary Butcher explicitly cites as inspirational, Pollard refers to the video work of Bill Viola, who 'describes treating visual images as if, like sound, they can penetrate the perceiving body and find "a resonant frequency latent in all spaces... a vital link between the unseen and the seen"'. Pollard signals the link with Butcher's visual concern, in *SCAN*, with 'material that flickers continuously with bursts of energy'.

   '[S]ome moments', Butcher argues, 'are more geared up to be memorable' than others, which has meant that she 'had to be exacting to duplicate sensation', which would contribute to a viewer's sense of a growing thematic focus, 'without repeating movement material'. At the same time, Pollard notes, decisions taken across a number of productions reveal the interrelations between them, which will, in terms of Butcher's ongoing enquiry, 'appear [to be] structured by Virilio's notion of exposure, rather than by notions of succession'. 'Exposure' is a poignant term, here. It can be applied to the performer, to the choreographer or visual artist, and, in fleeting moments, to a spectator's own engagement with the work. Sometimes the spectator's or the critic's response – that the work is too difficult, or too severe, or too ungiving – signals that her or his own tastes and prejudices have, in turn, been exposed by it. The 'structure of exposure' – in place of 'notions of [linear] succession' – informs this extended conversation between Pollard and Butcher, into which Pollard weaves her own observations of process.

In Janet Lansdale's essay, entitled 'Retrospective Insights, 1976-2001', the writer, one of the most important figures in Dance Studies in higher education and research in the UK, records some of her own impressions of Butcher's work. Lansdale enquires into the place Butcher's work has made for itself in dance over thirty years, asking how, in art historical terms, 'we see works of twenty-five years ago'. 'What kind of insight', she has written, 'do we bring compared to what a spectator in 1976 might have brought? Are such works in effect dead or alive for us?' Lansdale's essay, the writer points out, is less concerned with an art historical approach, however, than with 'the sense that [Butcher] focuses for a while on a group of inter-related issues and then moves on'. She may, indeed, loop back to them; hence it is difficult to establish a clear thematic or formal developmental sequence, neatly marked out by various periods of work made. Instead, Lansdale seems to suggest, there are issues, rather than forms as such, to which Butcher returns. Important amongst these 'is the issue of identity of the work and ownership. The role of improvisation and the responsibilities of the dancers have been a continuing motif throughout Rosemary Butcher's work'.

   According to Lansdale, citing Ramsay Burt,[1] Butcher's choreographic practices emerge from the attempt to communicate something through other people, to 'allow other people to say [in their way] what you want to say'. The power relations implicit in this observation are interesting, in the sense it gives that Butcher's work takes on board otherness (the dancer's expressivity) as constitutive of her own persona as artist.

COLLABORATORS
Clockwise from top left

Jim Fulkerson, RB, John Lyall

Simon Fisher-Turner

Cathy Lane and RB

Zaha Hadid

RB and Martin Otter

Michael Nyman, Dieter Pietsch and RB

Butcher's works as a whole, Lansdale suggests, pursue certain areas of aesthetic engagement, certain enquiries, in uncompromising terms, that dance in particular can facilitate, precisely because of its recourse to live human actions and interactions, performed in real time for present spectators. These concerns are not readily written about; they are not language-like, despite Butcher's metaphoric observation cited by Lansdale above. They are not limited to 'a narrowly conceived logic or a linearity of historical progression', because they 'seem to share characteristics of the dances themselves; the ideas, like the movement, loop back and forth, they return in a new way to familiar ground, they approach problems again and again but from yet another view'.

Lansdale's interest in what she calls these 'ideas', would seem to lead us to the consideration of 'ideas' as visual and figural, associative and spatially expansive, rather than writing-like, or indeed text-like: they 'loop', 'return', and 'approach... again', according to Lansdale. In the case of 'Flying Lines' (1985), it is explicitly, then, 'images that stimulated [the work]', in which one might identify 'a metaphor for a critical perspective', concerned with 'knotting, interlacing and veering off'.

Lansdale's impressions of Butcher's work, and of some of the writing it has prompted, are not unambiguous. Citing Jann Parry,[2] she confirms that it is 'only if you let her create the mood and determine the pace... [that] you come away rewarded'. Butcher's works, in Lansdale's terms, are not simply driven by ideas. Instead, they 'evoke a sensibility which has the potential to move fluidly between emotional and structural pathways'. In so doing, they touch, while also requiring of us that we work to understand the ways of seeing and doing that they propose.

It is worth noting, at this point, that Lansdale's perceptions are quite properly those specific to an *academic* expert spectator; as such, they are writing-productive, tend to be critical-analytical, and to that extent they also reveal the writerly preoccupations of the academic context. By way of contrast, Niki Pollard's text, written from the perspective of the rehearsal insider, attempts to articulate different presuppositions, different points of view with regard to 'practitioner', to 'process', to 'collaboration', and

to 'work'. From this different point (or points) of view, Niki Pollard's conclusion to writing about the rehearsal process in *SCAN* quotes Butcher in the following terms: 'Much of the piece is unaccountable to me. I do not know how I made those decisions, although they seemed absolutely right at the time. Like any piece, it is made up of a lot of mistakes and the decisions you forced because you could not get to where you wanted by any other means'.

Butcher adds, in Pollard's account: 'I allowed some things to be as there were enough of the things I wanted. If I wanted to keep a second instant, I had to keep the first even though I might not be able to account for why it was there. I was constantly questioning whether something should go or stay, but the fact of keeping it moving was more important than where it moved'. It is this quality of 'keeping it moving', rather than arriving somewhere (identifiable) that has tended to irritate, as well as to intrigue, some professional writers, who would prefer to be able to pin the work down.

Susan Leigh Foster's engagement with *SCAN* directly follows Pollard's enquiry and conversations with Rosemary Butcher. Foster's text *unfolds* material already explored – principally, thus far, from the perspective of Pollard's reflections on the rehearsal process. Foster's text attempts something quite particular, which is to introduce multiple perspectives into the single-authored text. Changing fonts in this particularly rich essay wilfully interrupt the conventional flow of writing, encouraging the sense that she views the work from a number of different perspectives, different points of view, different knowledge-bases. In this instance of what is called the parallax view (from the Greek word for 'alteration', which entails a change of position in relation to the object observed, a change in motion in the spectator herself), Foster is attempting to unfold, *in dancerly manner,* the complexities of Butcher's piece.

Susan Leigh Foster is a widely read academic analyst-interpreter of dance performance, with a particular interest in cultural theory and the registers and positions of dance writing. She asks whether 'we also find in *SCAN* a metaphor for new notions of the interface between human and machine?'

'The dancers in their pairings', she notes, who interrupt, assist and ghost one another, 'show us a new model for interactivity', displaying 'all our anxieties, but also the potential playfulness in these oncoming relations with smart houses and cars, with all forms of prostheses.' Her text provides detailed description of *what is there, what is happening* in the work – as if she wanted to give the piece itself the chance to speak its complexities*:*

> Dancers assist one another, supporting from behind as one falls backwards or sideways, pulling up from the floor to standing, jiggling shoulders as if to relieve tension, stroking the side of the head. But they also disrupt the path of another's motion; they block a gesture's momentum, entangle their own limb with the other body's activity. In these moments, caring assistance slides over into dominance: concern becomes control.

Detailed description is followed by developing abstraction and interpretation: 'Scanning, measuring, probing motions haunt the choreography'. In turn, we find biographical detail ('Returning to England in 1969, Butcher was hired by Dartington College to teach Graham technique, but she was hesitant to perpetuate its popularity') and cultural-historical detail ('Back in England, Graham's technique was just beginning to be deployed as an antidote to ballet. Its preference for bare-footed connection to the floor, for an exploration of surface-depth relations, opened radical new horizons of choreographic and training possibilities. What other technique came close to constituting itself so defiantly in opposition to the Pythagorean values of ballet?').

Foster ends her essay with an insight about choreographic practices which lifts her writing out of spectating, and into the sciences of performance-making: *SPAN*'s 'architectural and spatial sitedness, its materiality as movement, its disposition and coordination of physicalities, and its sequencing of events. These four choreographic elements are bound together in Butcher's work as intimately, complexly and elegantly as *SCAN*'s four dancers'.

What follows on from these two instances of experimental writing involves a further shift in perspective: Hugh Stoddart is a film-maker, screenwriter, dramatist and writer in visual arts, whose professional career has paralleled that of Rosemary Butcher. He describes himself as a reluctant follower of performances in designated spaces. Published in *Frieze* magazine, he wrote in November/December 1999, in his review of Breakwell and Geesin's *Auditorium*, at the ICA, London that 'I don't like joining an audience. Yet by the time I leave the theatre, as likely as not I'll have enjoyed myself. So why that initial resistance? Perhaps there's a feeling that something must be surrendered, like in the Westerns where you hand in your gun before entering the saloon. Is one's individuality threatened? One's privacy? Do I need protection?'

Certainly Stoddart provides a viewpoint in his essay on Butcher's work which is not specifically that of, nor limited to that of, the expert spectator *in performance:* her work reveals, instead, for Stoddart, a 'fine art sensibility', on which basis, 'Butcher pushes at the studio door', while 'remaining an impassioned devotee of the infinite possibilities of the human body as a source of expression'. Stoddart's essay is lighter in tone than some of those included here, more familiar, perhaps, with the struggles of a fellow artist, who 'notoriously' collaborates: 'I found out that [Butcher] now doubts "whether she has ever truly collaborated" – by which she means, I think, that she has never quite been in... a position of complete equality.'

Stoddart asserts, apparently lightly, echoing Janet Lansdale, that 'emotion [lies] within' Butcher's work. By implication, it needs, then 'to be exposed' – but by whom is it exposed? His essay certainly reinforces the sense that some artists, at least, are ready to acknowledge that they 'don't know what [they are] looking for until [they] find it', on which basis, once again, Stoddart adds, 'Butcher needs her dancers to be very generous, she needs them to be creative yet ready to surrender that creativity' to another's signature.

Stoddart remained particularly struck, at the time of writing, by Butcher's 1995 piece, *After the Last Sky*, which might be identified as one of her most political and least 'dancerly' works

NIGHT MOORING STONES
Prep and Filmimg Day, Dundee 1984

of the period, even though its visual aesthetic still depended on the input of dance artists: 'Because I thought this such a fine piece, and one which embodied both the dilemmas and the triumphs of Butcher's practice', Stoddart writes, he reproduces, in his essay, his review of *After the Last Sky,* published in *Frieze* no.21.

Josephine Leask provides the final, supporting insights into Rosemary Butcher's work, and the way it might be understood and interpreted. She argues that Butcher's claims 'to feel like an outsider' have given her a certain security, 'since it means that she is not in competition with others in the dance world', which has tended traditionally to 'prefer youth and beauty', to be 'competitive and ephemeral [by] nature', to be 'inward looking... encouraging artists to be both immature and self-obsessed'. By way of comparison, she notes, Rosemary Butcher 'feels more comfortable with the worlds of visual arts and architecture, which she argues both relate directly to real life'. Leask confirms something to which this collection of images and writing returns a number of times, which is that the developing aesthetic 'employed reduced movement with a focus on geometrical lines often made through skipping patterns and floor patterns of straight lines, right angles, arcs and circles'. On this basis, Leask points out, 'Butcher has described her early work as "a kinetic, sculptural experience" that drew the viewer's eye to body designs and group arrangements'. She cites Jordan's observation that in these early works 'the dancers were seen as distributions in space rather than single identities',[3] as well as that of Dodds, in *Dance Theatre Journal*, who adds that 'Butcher carefully constructs layers of movement so that slowly subtle textures and spatial patterns evolve'.[4] Leask links Butcher's characteristic thematics to 'minimal movement and open-endedness', '...evidenced in works which did not have a resolution and in which the dancers came and went, leaving impressions or traces behind them'.

Leask's text includes two short reviews, the first of the widely viewed and much written about *SCAN*, and the second of the relatively under-reviewed collaborative *d2* (1989-90), part of the D-Tryptych, performed in Spitalfields Cathedral, East London.

d2 was 'a collaboration with architect John Lyall and composer Jim Fulkerson', Leask notes, and the piece was site-specific, with 'the nave... turned into a performance space with high catwalks down each aisle', on which dancers appeared,'moving their arms very slowly, while other dancers ran down the nave swinging their arms vigorously, alternating between running and walking'.

What Leask finally emphasises here is Butcher's capacity, even in the mid-period work, to conjure up, in spectators and listeners, a sense of something (abstract) which it could not actually represent: in Leask's words, a sense of 'solemnity', for example, emerged through the layering of action in differently located dancers, within this resonant architectural complex; with the addition of Fulkerson's score, the whole work seemed to be 'gradually rising to the sublime'.

In my own long, concluding essay, I attempt to reflect on Butcher's most recent work by juxtaposing it against a philosophical text originally published in French in 1970, the precise period when Rosemary Butcher's identity as a working artist began to take (public) shape. The text – Gilles Deleuze's *Spinoza: Practical Philosophy,* curiously not published in English until 1988[5] – cannot be said to have 'influenced Butcher'. Rather, something in them can be said to have coincided. In my argument, both took up, in speculative manner, *something in the air*, which each sensed, and measured, and rearticulated, in different ways – and in ways which can be called signature-specific.

Deleuze's little book provides me with a sense of the ways the material can be used to do more than it actually does. It provides something of an analogy with choreographic and visual art real-time-based practices of a challenging kind, in the precise sense that Deleuze's text takes up and reconfigures another philosophical text (written around three hundred years earlier). Deleuze's text uses words and phrases used by Spinoza in the 1670s, although these have gone through a number of processes of translation. However, time, as well as understandings, has moved on.

Something seems, nonetheless, to remain, to have crystallised;

ROSEMARY
SOLO DUO
1981

to reappear on the page, almost *as itself*; but that 'something', equally, has been relayed, re-appraised, differently positioned, reviewed through inevitably different frameworks. It differently resonates, pleases differently – or it no longer pleases. In Butcher's work 'dance', or, in fact, *dancers*, appear, they retreat, and they reappear, differently observed. Where they differ most notably from text, from a 'language', from words, is in the singularity of the human individual whose work is choreographed, in order to be looked at, and turned, and turned again, and looked at again. They bear that look, that quality of the twice-looked-at, of theatricality itself. They enable Butcher to look carefully at something, to conjure something up, to put it on show, to take it back. Dance and choreography loop back, taking what they have learnt (from doing/showing it) with them, and allow those of us who are spectators, sometimes quite suddenly, to look differently at other instances of their disciplinary tradition. And dance – unlike texts, or words, or paintings, indeed – looks back at us.

Endnotes

1   Burt, R. 'Finding a Language', *New Dance*, 44, Summer 1988, pp.12-14

2   Parry, J. 'Butcher alone', *The Observer*, May 25, 1986, p.19

3   Ibid. p.172

4   S. Dodds, 'The momentum continues', *Dance Theatre Journal*, Volume 13 (X), 1997, pp.6-9

5   G. Deleuze, *Spinoza: Practical Philosophy*, trans. R.Hurley, San Francisco: City Lights Books, 1988 (first published in the French as *Spinoza: Philosophie pratique*, Presses Universitaires de France, 1970)

ROSEMARY BUTCHER

SILENT SPRING
Research. Film: Chris Welsby, 1989

SILENT SPRING
Research. Film: Chris Welsby, 1989

SHELL; FORCE FIELDS AND SPACES 1982

TCR 02:08:19:12

TCR 01:08:23:06

TCR 02:05:14:12

OF SHADOWS AND WALLS 1991

If distinctiveness is a necessary part of talent, and persistence indispensable for achieving recognition, Rosemary Butcher should by now be basking centre stage. That she is not is a measure of her refusal to compromise. She certainly has both the capacity as an artist and the persistence, while her distinctiveness is such that it places her in a unique position. This distinctiveness comes not so much from the movement she creates – although that in itself has a lucidity that is remarkable – but in the way she has dissolved boundaries to hover between dance and visual art, leaning now more toward the one, now more toward the other. Her dancework is close to kinetic installation; it avoids conventional theatres in favour of outdoor spaces, art galleries or even flexible performance studios. You could legitimately ask whether it is actually dance or an art exhibit with live performers. That it might be both has seemed to disturb some critics and spectators uneasy with hybrid genres and with performance modes which don't slot into familiar compartments.

Hybridisation apart, spectators may feel free to reject someone whose own dance language tends to reject established convention. If Butcher avoids conventional theatres, it is not just to reinforce the complexity of her art, but also to signal that difference lies at the centre of her work. If theatres carry in-built preconceptions about 'meaning', structural progression and performers who play to their audience – and they tend to do so – Butcher was marked as a student in the late 1960s-1970s, by the ideas of American postmodern dance, which held, among other things, that dance *could be* about nothing but itself, that real time (freewheeling, non-developmental)

ROSEMARY BUTCHER: A CRITICAL OVERVIEW, 2000

NADINE MEISNER

could belong on stage and that everyday movement itself provided a valid performance vocabulary. Butcher set herself constraints that would identify her with the postmodern or the minimalist and has, more or less, stayed with these throughout her professional career. She rarely builds a sense of impetus, let alone deliberate progressions, climaxes or resolutions. Her movement phrases appear, disappear and reappear without necessarily seeming joined up. Her early work introduced lots of stopping and starting and walking. Equally, it revealed that these movement phrases might be repeated and modified as to angle or location, but never expanded or elaborated. Finally, she is very particular about the way her performers appear: they have a normal-body stance and their movement is naturalistic, alerting the viewer to the beauty of ordinariness. They signal neutral self-containment, as though unaware that they are being watched. They turn the tables on spectators, who themselves need to take on the extra distance to make contact. Thirty years on, these principles seem commonplace, absorbed to a greater or lesser degree into contemporary dance. But at the time they caused extreme difficulty with a public expecting a 'performance', and even now the mainstream remains resistant when faced with them in such concentrated form.

Butcher was an independent before the independent choreographic artist became fashionable in Britain. Enrolled in the newly opened dance course at Dartington College of the Arts, in South Devon, supplemented with stints at the London School of Contemporary Dance, she spent the year following her graduation (1968) with a scholarship in the USA, studying Doris Humphrey technique, and attending the Graham and the Cunningham studios. Shortly before her return to Britain, she witnessed the work of Yvonne Rainer, Steve Paxton and other contemporary artists who gave concerts at the Judson Church in New York. Back in Britain, teaching at Dartington, she began to digest the implications of what she had seen. She went to New York again in 1970, just to watch in earnest, and when in 1972 she returned home, Butcher reports that she felt that British dance culture was ten years out of date.

Rosemary Butcher was the first British choreographer to absorb the ideas of the Judson Church postmodern artists, although others followed her later. Moreover, unlike some of her compatriots, she has never forged close ties to a central institution like the Contemporary Dance Trust in London. Dartington was located, artistically as well as geographically, on the fringes and she herself lacked the inclination to align herself with an established company or ideologically driven collective. At a time when independent artists were a rarity, she acknowledged that this made life difficult, but in the long term, it has preserved her artistic integrity, protecting her from the compromises of dealing with communal responsibilities and conflicting visions.

Rosemary Butcher made her choreographic debut in 1974 with *Uneven Time*, made for Scottish Ballet's Moveable Workshop. It featured apparently banal plucking and smoothing hand gestures, walks and runs in lines and circles. In 1976, she started her own intermittent group, the Rosemary Butcher Dance Company. Her choreographic precepts were reinforced by the influence of other Americans now at Dartington College – Steve Paxton, a proponent of the egalitarian partnership skills of contact improvisation, and Mary Fulkerson, a teacher of the stress-free body awareness of release technique. Like other artists of the time, she made outdoor pieces. *Passage North East* (1976) was shown in several places, among them the piazza outside London's Economist building. Office staff passing by were incorporated into the performance. The dancing, accompanied only by the surrounding city noise, embraced improvisational elements within set structures.

The performers wore sneakers, a reaction against the barefoot modern dancer, emphasising the deliberate simplicity and functionality of Butcher's movement. This included, as Butcher remembers, 'a strange sort of skipping step'. Her preoccupation then was not so much about movement shapes, but about geometries in space – the invisible lines between dancers and their surroundings. In presenting a given piece in different locations, she was highly sensitive to the impact of the surroundings. 'It was important that the environment should become part of it,' she remembers, 'the bend in a river, a particular roof, people looking out of windows.'

Although originally derivative, Butcher's investigation was soon to take a distinctive turning. In 1978, she became resident choreographer at Riverside Studios in London, which together with an Arts Council grant gave her strong creative stimulus. She made six pieces that year: *Theme*, a group piece, was set against photographic slides by Darryl Williams, as was *Uneven Time*, a solo for Maedée Duprès (which shared its title with a piece Butcher made in 1974). Duprès, in a play of stillness and motion, would move in front of her static photographic image or freeze when these images were flicked in quick succession. Other works included *Anchor Relay* (shown on a double bill with *Theme*); *Touch and Go*, significantly dependent on contact improvisation; and *Catch 5, Catch 6*, a choreographic game that allowed choices within its rules. These were 'sneaker pieces' and many were physically dynamic.

Rosemary Butcher points out that the year at Riverside was less significant for what she choreographed than for the two visual artists that she met, Jon Groom and Heinz Dieter Pietsch. This encounter can be seen, with hindsight, to have had a seminal influence on the direction of her work. It made it highly particular: no-one else had pursued the fusion of artistic forms to such elaborate, sophisticated lengths. It is only in recent years that a new generation such as Boris Charmatz (France) and Frederick Flamand (Belgium) has

IMAGES EVERY THREE SECONDS 2003

explored similar territory. In Butcher's case it has produced work that is extraordinary in its originality, subtle detail and delicate atmosphere. She started in 1980, with the popular *Five-sided Figure*, by which time her Riverside residency had ended and she had returned to teach at Dartington.

The fact that the piece included music was not unusual (she had used music before), but Jon Groom devised a pentagon floor figure, bounded by screens. Butcher was a member of the cast along with Janet Smith, Julyen Hamilton and Sue MacLennan and remembers her choreography as 'working with edges', while other accounts suggest a rounded, flowing aesthetic in contrast to Groom's angular forms. Either way, the collaboration inspired Butcher to think about the shape of movement. This preoccupation continued with *Shell: Force Fields and Spaces* (1981), to a score by Jim Fulkerson. 'Jon set up the premise of the shell, so everything to do with the piece was circular – the movement, the whole thing moved in spirals,' Butcher recalls. 'I started the piece with a solo, in a spot in the middle, while a trombone played. I just went round and round in improvised circles.' Again screens circumscribed a space where light projections drew changing circles, segments of circles and radii.

The collaborations with Pietsch were closer, Pietsch making a point of attending rehearsals. In the first of these, *Spaces 4* (1981), the white-clothed, animate silhouettes of the four dancers extended and overlapped with Pietsch's similarly white, inanimate shapes. Broken-edged, these resembled lower pieces of walls and corners and hinted at four squares,

like remnants of lost rooms. 'I was beginning to see the possibilities of bodies, texture and layering, all treated abstractly,' Butcher recently observed. 'The piece had sections, but it was basically improvised with the dancers given set things to do'. Barefoot, they moved with intent slowness in the still silence, halting, crouching, replacing each other, giant Henry Moore figures against Lilliputian wall fragments. However, in its hermetic insularity, this piece still belongs with Butcher's early blanched works, where emotional resonance is barred and the effect clinical.

Where pieces like *Passage North East* had focused on the body's direction in space, Butcher was now increasingly concerned with the body's own contours. She further developed this enquiry with two companion pieces in 1983, *The Site* and *Imprints*. The dancers' physicality seemed intensely vivid, yet at the same time they were integrated in Pietsch's setting, an effect enhanced by Malcolm Clarke's tapes of elemental sound, incorporating distant wind and vibrations. The different components coalesced into an organic and highly atmospheric whole. These can be described as contemplative pieces, immersing not only the performers, but also the spectators.

Butcher's ideas may have originally been linked to her experience of the work of her American predecessors, but *The Site* and *Imprints* marked her singularity. By now she was creating her movement through the dancers' improvisations, prompted by precise instructions or tasks. This has been her method ever since: she sees what the dancers offer her, and if the result isn't what she wants, she will refine or change her instruction, but not actually declare nor demonstrate what she wants, the rule being that it has to originate in what the dancers come up with. In other words, like Pina Bausch, she draws up the grand plan, channels the dancers' improvisations, and applies her editorial eye to sift and structure the resulting material.

The working theme for *The Site* was an archaeological dig, its terminology, tasks and images. The performance itself also provided room for structured improvisation, cues allowing the performers (Gaby Agis, Dennis Greenwood, Helen Rowsell and Miranda Tufnell) to react to each other. If a dancer moved to a corner, for example, he or she had to perform 'post-holing' movements and this in turn gave permission to anyone of the other dancers to fall to the ground. The improvisation was not easily grasped by the spectator, unless he or she could remember a previous performance. Nor could it contain any surprises for Butcher, since it allowed only responses from a limited range of possibilities. Why include it? Perhaps it was merely an ideological statement, an avant-badge?

IMAGES EVERY THREE SECONDS 2003

Perhaps that was part of it, given that her later pieces have been more set. But she also argues that it gave these particular performances a one-off edge, because the dancers had to keep their minds constantly alert.

You might not identify the piece as concerned with excavation, although as spectator you would be aware of the closeness to the ground. More probably, you would see timeless people in a timeless environment, engaged in some alien, inscrutable, even disturbing activity, sometimes lying with an ear to the earth as if listening, or standing watchfully as if feeling some hidden force. The piece 'goes nowhere', but the mysterious ambience created by the work draws you in. Pietsch's contribution involved low irregular mounds like topographical contours seen from far above and – unexpectedly – neon strips casting an eerie blue-white light. Sometimes the performers would droop themselves over the neon strips, strange figures in dislocated behaviour, the light picking out their muscles and bones.

For *Imprints* (again containing structured improvisation), Pietsch constructed two irregular, derelict screens divided by a gap. Butcher apparently imagined imprints as a close-up fragment of *The Site*: Dennis Greenwood and Gaby Agis would enter, exit and pause slowly to imprint their silhouettes. Butcher saw one imprint as sometimes superimposing itself on another and replacing it, creating the effect of one person repeatedly slipping away from the other, or being protected. At one performance, Agis's body pressed against the back wall between the screens, one arm raised; Greenwood was

alongside her, his head bent into her neck, producing an image of intense vulnerability. The performers executed these poses as if they were emotional blanks, yet, unlike *Spaces 4*, the effect was quite different.

The noncommittal performing style and Butcher's refusal to direct the spectator's responses were to produce a distinctive impact in all subsequent work. What a spectator sees is expressive but, at the same time, ambiguous. What you might make of an image is up to you; the resonances exist in each spectator's mind. Equally distinctive are the repercussions of the choreography's minimalist simplicity. If the American postmodern taught us anything, it was to look at ordinary, unassuming movement and see its beauty. Understatement invites the spectator to sharpen his or her perception and to notice details previously overlooked. The low-key shuffles and immobility of *The Site* require a process of winding down, the opposite of dramatic overkill.

Heightened by their setting and sound scores, *The Site* and *Imprints* stand out as consummate achievements of movement and of strange, suppressed drama. Butcher has always favoured a frugal directness, not as a matter of doctrine, but instead of the attempt to hold on to the humanity of movement. The leakage of emotion perceived at this stage of the work was involuntary, but it was nevertheless a side-effect that she could see. After *Spaces 4*, she made no attempt to erase it. Perhaps she had become aware that without that human dimension, art tends to become mechanical. Perhaps that is why she has never followed the full 'systems' route pursued by purist minimalists like Lucinda Childs. Butcher has observed that she admired Childs's early works in which set mathematical schemes elaborated spatial patterns through deliberately limited movement. She has tried on occasions to emulate her work and has often used systems to some degree. Butcher observes, however, that a time always came in making a given piece, when she felt like she couldn't stick to a single system because she didn't like what was emerging.

The 1982 solo for Sue MacLennan, *Field Beyond Maps*, was one piece where Butcher applied a system, but without the same constraints. It had the speed and directional geometry of a Childs piece. 'I'm sure it was hugely influenced by her diagonals and their purity, but I was more complex in the way I used the body', remembers Butcher. Complexity here has to be understood as signifying variety, rather than overt virtuosity. By then most minimalists, including Childs, were turning away from naturalistic movement in favour of an overt dancerly athleticism, but Butcher stood against this current, keeping to basic dynamics, such as running, turning and skipping.

TOUCH THE EARTH, prep work
Venice and Wimbledon Common 1987

TOUCH THE EARTH
Whitechapel Gallery 1987

Field Beyond Maps was premiered between the shape-orientated Groom and Pietsch pieces. Like many artists, Butcher swings between approaches, so that even while her work shows a general trend forward there are still occasional reversions to previous modes and an evident desire, after exploring one mode, to find relief in another. The movement of other systems-influenced pieces like *Flying Lines* (1985) and the *d1*, *d2* and *3D* trilogy (1989-1990) bisected space in the same way. That linked them with early pieces like *Passage North East*. But in addition, they included a characteristic drive and patterning, pushed by rhythmically insistent music. Using eight dancers, *Flying Lines* was the first of Butcher's large-scale pieces, to a lushly layered piano score commissioned from and played by Michael Nyman. For her theme, she turned to kite-flying, then enjoying a revival, so that the movement went backwards and forwards and looped. The piece started slowly, with two dancers lying face down. As the action gradually developed, so the choreography built into criss-crossing diagonals of walking and running, arms semaphoring, or into wheeling arcs backwards and forwards. The systems template was evident, but Butcher deliberately broke it up.

In playing the piano, Michael Nyman would wait for cues from the dancers, with the option of going with or against the movement's pre-arranged tempo. At one performance in Paris, he played faster and faster because he wanted to get away to watch a football match and it is reported that the dancers had difficulty keeping up. The lighting suggested

was that one half of the piece represented night, the other day. For the design, Butcher had wanted to work with Pietsch again, but because he wasn't available, Peter Noble, who shared his studio, devised suspended fabric structures that resembled tattered flags. 'It looked wonderful lit because of the height of these things', Butcher recalls. 'They filled the space and the light came behind you and had these figures whirling on the ground.'

Because of its exhilarating accumulation of rhythmic impetus, *Flying Lines* could be argued to have been an accessible if rather superficial piece that became popular with audiences and critics. *d1*, *d2* and *3D*, three distinct but linked collaborations with the architects Zaha Hadid (*d1*), and John Lyall (*d2*, *3D*) were again semi-systems, pattern pieces impelled by the strong rhythms of Jim Fulkerson's scores and concerned with energetic lines that were continuous or fractured.

Although the previous piece, *Touch the Earth* (1987), had the same size cast and included a system mid-way, it was more contemplative. It again featured music by Nyman, while Pietsch made not only screens but rods like abstracted evocations of ancient weapons or farming implements. The initial idea had been the wooden posts that mark out the navigation channels in the Bay of Venice. This initial idea fanned out into notions of boundaries, land, colonisation and loss of ownership. Butcher's thinking included the plight of Native Americans; while Nyman focused on Goethe's description of Venetians calling to each other across the water. He composed music for singers and Alexander Balanescu's string quartet which meant that the performances were equally important musical events. The score occupied a more decisive place, obliging Butcher to adjust her structures to it, and pulling the piece together in unforeseen ways. 'Women's voices call to each other over vast, watery distances,' *The Observer*'s reviewer wrote (31 January 1988):

> …an intent procession of figures moves across the space, some carrying bronze spears or poles with which they stake out their territory. Rosemary Butcher's choreography for *Touch the Earth* is beautiful and haunting in its sense of desolation, of a perpetual journeying without any destination.

The desolate mood became even more pronounced in *After the Crying and the Shouting* (1989). Where earlier in her work emotional expressivity had been an involuntary, but unsuppressed, side-product, here Butcher knowingly opted to infuse the work with a sense of underlying emotion, working with elements and tasks that would enable the spectator to sense this. As such, the piece (to music by Wim Mertens) represents a milestone. Created after her father's death and inspired, among other things by T.S. Eliot's *The Wasteland*, its themes were loss and death. But Ron Haselden's overhead tangle of fairy lights contributed to a prettiness at odds with the emotionality, and the piece never quite seemed to gel. Butcher reacted by swinging back to spatial patterning in the *d1*, *d2* and *3D* trilogy that followed, although she has recently indicated an interest in returning to it.

Meanwhile, film was creeping into her work. Butcher had originally wanted to include film in *After the Crying and the Shouting*, but even earlier, in *Night Mooring Stones* (1984), she had used landscape footage by Jane Rigby as a way of enlarging the context and bringing the outdoors indoors. Performed only once, it was a sketch towards the consummate *Unbroken View: Extended Frame* (1995). Butcher argues that film is particularly apt for dealing with notions of memory and dimensions of time, and Sigune Hamann's bleached, fragmented projections in *Unbroken View* appeared like a crystallisation of memory, with all its partialities and exaggerations. Butcher recalls now that 'the piece definitely was concerned with the past and how things got exaggerated by memory'. 'The images were grainy and sometimes they were like still photographs. Or sometimes they were upside down. Or again, sometimes they dealt with rooms and peering into things that weren't clear.' They included a recurring image of a train, hurtling along like time itself, and all the while the projector made a clicking noise, like old home movies. Juxtaposed with the choreography, it evoked the dreamlike quality of the choreography's manic repetitions, arrested moments and sleeping postures.

In this piece and the next, *Fractured Landscapes, Fragmented Narratives* (1997), Butcher observes that 'a real extremism was coming into the images through an exaggeration of pushing of physical forms', and that this itself produced a sense of emotional intensity. *Fractured Landscapes* took film technology into the sophisticated terrain of mixing actual performers with video images that were sometimes pre-recorded, sometimes 'live' – that is, filmed and immediately relayed with just a fractional time lag. Before these two pieces, Butcher achieved an even more radical enterprise: *After the Last Sky* (1995), a film installation in collaboration with Noel Bramley, the title taken from a text by Edward Said. Four twenty-minute long films were projected on the walls of a specially constructed, boxed space. On one wall was an orange and red sky, on each of the others, a different dancer almost life-size, in black and white. To Simon Fisher's score of sounds recorded in Israel, Jonathan Burrows, Dennis Greenwood, Russell Maliphant, Fin Walker, Deborah Jones and Gill Clarke performed pared-down movement around the spectator – tying a shoelace, lurching into a handstand, hitching up trousers – one dancer counterpointing the work of the other.

The repetition, deliberation and proximity to the watcher of these simple actions accentuated their humanity. They became utterly beautiful. It didn't matter that the intended theme of confinement – individuals caught in time, people in exile, contrasting with the limitless sky – was too oblique to be apparent. Butcher has observed that 'it seemed I was dealing

TOUCH THE EARTH
Whitechapel Gallery 1987

with human situations and predicaments more and more'. She reports now, however, that she found the absence of live performers in *After the Last Sky* trying, and was doubtful about the way the film footage recorded only the edited highlights of movement phrases. Yet in concept the piece was unique and its technology almost perfect – even if some sections of the public and press were unimpressed. The work premiered at the Royal College of Art in London, and Butcher describes it as the closest she has come to exhibiting dance as visual art, to be viewed from any point in the space, the video reels always restarting themselves after the end.

Away from film, *Body as Site* (1992-3), created three years earlier, also seamlessly merged dance and visual art. It did not, however, achieve the same culmination of form, given that it still used live dancers and conventional time limits, and as such retained the framework of a performance. Performed in art galleries and consisting of four separate sections, it required spectators to move from one section to the other as an audience, not as strolling visitors. Even so, each section to a greater or lesser degree communicated the sense of an exhibit, of something simply present, in which the moving body was an integral part of the artistic vision, so that it was impossible to tell which was the context – the body or the artwork. But where for the Pietsch pieces the process had consisted of an equal, parallel consultation between choreographer and artist, for *Body as Site*, Butcher retrospectively complied with each artist's defined vision. For the first item, 'Tracer', Paul Elliman invented a floor-grid

of cats' eyes and, on the walls, photographs of the dancers, so the handstanding, darting dancers were counterpointing and echoing their still images. In 'The Wasp', Ron Hasleden used a lamp and rotating shape to project a big yellow sun and cloud onto the floor, overlooked by a mirror hanging at an angle and vibrating to the sound of buzzing. For the choreography, Butcher decided to use a solo, *Desert Pieces*, that she had already been working on with dancer Gill Clarke. The dynamic of this figure, pacing or shifting about in imaginary sand, collided with the sound and light to produce an effect of entrapment, of being pinned under a scorching sun.

Butcher observed that at first, she felt she couldn't use the four curved boards, strung with rope, that architect John Lyall devised for the third section, 'Tension and Compression'. But eventually the capacity to rock the boards and hold the ropes sparked associations: 'It conjured up so much, I amazed myself,' Butcher recalls. 'I was being pushed on by the limitations into realms [where] I wouldn't normally have gone'. The boards were moved around, lined up. They became reminiscent of sails or boats, conjured up a hidden narrative of cooperation, a sea journey and maybe even a rescue.

Most dramatically evocative, however, was the finale, 'Recover', with Anya Gallacio's expanse of white horsehair. It lay like a giant cumulus cloud eiderdown, while the impassive dancers, dressed in what might have been pyjamas, could only fall, hop and lie if they were to avoid entangling their feet in the horsehair. Those restrictions threw up extraordinary pictures: were the dancers angels or sleepers? They hopped in arabesques and attitudes, they lifted each other and suspended each other in frozen off-balance poses. The slow oceanic music emphasised the slowness of the movement. And when Dennis Greenwood lay in a crucifix position, or Gill Clarke placed a hand on Greenwood's shoulder, or Clarke walked on Greenwood's prostrate body, you saw again how in a delicate, understated context, certain developments could acquire the proportions of a thunderclap.

It takes more, however, than external restrictions or happy

accident to produce such resonances. It takes a masterly eye to direct dancers' improvisations, then to edit and structure them to produce such unforgettable movement threads that break, recur and link up with other sequences. It takes a real gift to seek out images rich with possible associations and adjust them to the context so that they strike deep evocative chords in the viewer. Each item in *Body as Site* is honed like a priceless exhibit.

Body as Site and *After the Last Sky* featured some of Butcher's longest dancer-collaborators: Jonathan Burrows, Gill Clarke, Fin Walker and especially Dennis Greenwood. If they have stayed with her over the years, clearly it is because they admire her work, and she in turn likes the individual baggage they bring with their maturity. Yet her influence on the dance profession has finally been more as a teacher, less as a choreographer. With the possible exception of Burrows – and even there the stylistic connections seem tangential – no-one has yet followed in her footsteps; even the recent fusions of art and dance from abroad are, it would appear, independent initiatives.

Some observers would maintain that she not only occupies the margins, but labours in a dead end. I would argue to the contrary that perhaps the most impressive aspect of her work is the way she has an identifiable style which never becomes formulaic. Despite the frugality of her grammar, each piece involves a fresh process of discovery; each has its own movement texture. This development continued with the millennial piece, *SCAN* (2000). Inspired by the processes of human physiology, *SCAN* not only sustained her commitment to collaborate with other artistic forms – in this case sound and film – but renewed her enthusiasm for partnering. Early on, with *Landings* (1976) and *Spaces Between* (1977), both for Maedée Duprès and Julyen Hamilton, she had transformed this traditional form into a highly lucid

possible articulation of shape and structure. (*Landings* in fact won a Royal Society of Arts prize which financed another trip to the USA in 1978.) In *SCAN*, she not only resumed partnering with two simultaneous and interchanging couples, but, typically, gave the work an entirely new dimension, enriching the movement with dense reference points to human physicality and to sculptural shape. That is the essence of Butcher's work: always true to herself, never compromising, but at the same time always searching into the future.

TOUCH THE EARTH
Company & friends, Whitechapel Gallery 1987

TOUCH THE EARTH
Whitechapel Gallery 1987

WHITE FIELD 1977

WHITE FIELD 1977

The Wasp
BODY AS SITE 1993
Ron Haselden

COLLISIONS AND COLLABORATIONS

ROBERT AYERS IN CONVERSATION WITH ROSEMARY BUTCHER, 2001

What follows is not a simple transcription of an interview. Instead, it records a conversation in which two practising artists explore where they might find common terrain. Robert Ayers is an English-born, Manhattan-based performance artist, who until recently was Professor of Contemporary Arts at Nottingham Trent University, UK. In 2003 he was awarded funding, on the basis of academic excellence, to work directly with Martha Wilson at Franklin Furnace for four months, making an extended study of the current relationship between digital and live performance, and using the current Franklin Furnace *Fund for Performance Art* and *Future of the Present* projects as case studies. He is particularly interested in the point at which the live and the digital meet. Robert Ayers is a widely published writer, teacher and curator. His words are represented below, in bold.

Robert Ayers: **To what extent do you feel that collaboration is something that comes automatically in the sphere of dance?**

RB: Not in the way that I think I've resolved it. I think that dance has, in part, inherently existed with other media, but there have always been additional theatrical mechanisms: for instance, dance historically has always found its place with sound and music. Early on in my choreography those things weren't relevant to me.

I didn't feel that sound was necessary when I started to do my own work.

I had a very traditional training in Britain until I studied at Dartington and in New York. And then, for some reason, it seems as though I've taken an attitude towards dance that collides with visual art. People have told me that what I do is quite painterly. Certainly, the process is about making images happen as on paper or in sculpture, rather than creating prescribed movement.

You work with artists from other media, but there hasn't been a point at which the collaboration has resulted in something other than dance. It doesn't become interdisciplinary in the wrong sense – a cross-disciplinary messy kind of thing that you can't recognise.

RB: Because of the way in which I work and the nature of the collaboration, the identity of the work – whose work it is – can be quite problematic. But this worries me less as time goes on. I think it is legitimate to bring someone in because you feel that they are going to enhance what you do. In some cases visual artists don't actually make their own work anymore, but it is their concept. Within dance, for a long time, even using improvisation or getting dancers to develop their own material was in some way letting the side down. I think that has been a battle for me.

But I still desperately want to control the form – and the dancers and the other collaborators have to somehow be interested in allowing their input to be part of a shared process. It has to be reciprocal.

What I find interesting is that, in the end, I desperately need the support of other people; it is their support that makes the work so much richer, sometimes because of the energy that comes out of different disciplines coming together.

In *SCAN* (2000), there's not much there that you would identify as lighting design or costume design in traditional terms; it is far more like a collision between two artistic intelligences.

RB: It has happened before, for example with John Lyall in the 'Tension and Compression' section of *Body as Site* (1992-93). For that piece, I asked four artists to give me four environments and John provided four nine-foot MDF boards with struts. When he brought them in, it was just chaos! It was like a seventies theatre workshop; the dancers were getting stupid running up and down the boards and making them rock back and forth like a see-saw. I rang John and I said: 'I can't work with these boards. There's nothing emerging and I have nothing to work with.' Then I thought I'd just use one of them and just use the idea, and that was the key. I didn't get rid of them. John just lit the boards and

Image as Event
BODY AS SITE 1993
Artist: Paul Elliman

they provided a sense of a boundary, a sense of a tent, a sense of a building. They conjured up a sense of another world for me. I also took something about the boards and their tension and compression for the dancers' bodies, which is something very particular and direct.

I gave all four artists – Paul Elliman, Ron Haselden, Anya Gallacio and John Lyall – the same problem of creating an environment for me and therefore I had to accept the premise of what they were giving me. With Anya Gallacio's and John's designs, less so with the other two, I actually had to work with a different type of choreography to match the given environments.

The one section that wasn't choreographically informed was Anya Gallacio's 'clouds' of cotton fibre. The environment restricted me so much that I had to make the movement very simple. Interestingly, it worked in the context of the whole piece. I accepted that it was one of four parts. Maybe, even without the cotton fibre, I would have made that decision in the end. Perhaps I would have created something very simple at that stage in the piece anyway.

John Lyall loved being part of the collaborative process. John and I were interviewed for an article in the architecture magazine *Blueprint* about our collaboration, and it was quite interesting hearing our views. John provided me with a vehicle but John discovered some creative inspiration from our collaboration.

To what extent do you think your attitude towards collaboration derives from your experience of Judson?

RB: Not at all.

Not at all? That's interesting.

RB: I think I was influenced by the things that were happening around me in New York at that time, not just by the choreography. I don't think any of the Judson choreographers dealt with form in the same way as I do. I felt that I was much more concerned with structure than any of them. I always felt that I was going backwards. I thought that they were much more radical than I was. I wanted to be radical but I never felt that I was. To me they were my pin-ups; the people that you think you will never be.

When did you go to New York?

RB: 1967. I met Alex and Deborah Hay in New York, and I spent a lot of time with them.

Deborah worked on some pieces that I went to see that she did in her loft with a plank of wood. People had to walk along the plank, but if the plank moved then they would take two steps back. This went on for hours. No-one got to the end of the plank. I have never forgotten it. That was truly radical for the time.

I developed those ideas into something that I feel is more concrete. I was conscious of form

and I was conscious of adding it back into my other influences and then putting them into a context that was the one I wanted. It wasn't just about presenting a series of things that were experimental.

When you say form do you mean physical form, choreographic form, spatial form?

RB: Definitely! I'm not sure that 'form' is the right term and it's probably not fashionable. It is the idea of things pertaining to each other. I keep changing the nature of the structure of what it might be that things are pertaining to. It doesn't matter what rules there are within the form – it's about what is holding the piece together.

The expression 'things pertaining to each other' is something which seems very important to your work. You've collaborated with many different people but the work is identifiably yours throughout. There is a kind of personality, a kind of atmosphere, a kind of spirit which is there throughout the work. Part of the secret of your success in your collaborations is that the level at which the collaboration is intended to function is one in which the sculpture and the dance are allowed to speak their own languages – but they're talking about the same sort of subject.

In Spaces Four (1981), for example, the degree to which

the choreography has a relationship with Heinz-Dieter Pietsch's sculpture is a question of the sculpture never stopping being sculpture and the choreography never stopping being choreography. There is a shared subject rather than a shared language. Yet you said that you work in a painterly way. What do you mean by that?

RB: It comes from other people commenting on watching me work – that I come in to rehearsal with nothing other than the idea of saying something that will create something else, with only an abstract concept. I have no preconception of what the final work will be. I deal with what comes up, and keep dealing with what comes up, until I find somehow that the original concept collides with the information that I'm giving in response to what I'm getting back from the dancers.

You seem to be describing a pragmatic, experimental process.

RB: I'll see something and I'll put that down in my memory or go back to the preparation and refer to and add to the preparation. Then I'll take away and add on again to the material, throwing in things all the time, to take the performer away from the present. I do that by almost attacking what I've set up.

The degree with which you collaborate with individual dancers makes them become

important to you.

RB: You fall in love with them because they are manifesting something you can't get to in any other way. They can't not be very special. I can let go when I am not working but it's very important that the relationship doesn't get lost. It's only developed badly on one or two occasions. On the whole there's always something that has gone on existing with a dancer, even without the working relationship, and that's good.

I think one of the things that is worth saying about your work is the extent to which your relationship with the dancers is non-collaborative. You work with them on pieces of movement but at the end of the day it's the Rosemary Butcher Dance Company and you get to make the final choices. At the same time you carry the can. You are the one who is praised or criticised.

RB: I think that's what I want. I can't deny it. I've been challenged on occasions by my own dancers about my ego, but I still believe I'm more interested in my work than I am in myself. I wouldn't want any poor work to go out, but I have done a lot of shows where I have lost dancers to illness or injury and I have had to still carry on. But I suppose I carry the can because I enjoy the responsibility.

Whenever I've worked with companies creating art performances, one of the real

strains was having to maintain their interest when they're not aware that anything is happening.

RB: I think people who have worked with me on one or two projects know in the end that we tend to get there even if it is at the last minute.

There's always a prickly time where people are moving away from you or are feeling left out – especially if you are not coming up with the goods as quickly as they would like. For the dancers, it's often about the meaning of a project that they can tell people to come and see. One of the dancers I have worked with waited until the dress rehearsal before he invited his friends – to be sure there was something for them to see.

That's the attitude of the old Soviet space programme. They wouldn't tell anyone they'd been to the moon until they'd already been there.

RB: That's very much it, and that's not easy to work with. But I can get through that because part of the process in the end is the very thing that you're grappling with – your idea and the dancers' connection to it.

In your work, you have to deal with deadlines. It's a very risky process – you're throwing these ideas together with an artist, or an artist and a composer and a group of dancers and there has to be a process of resolution.

Recover
BODY AS SITE 1993
Artist: Anya Gallacio

Image as Event
BODY AS SITE 1993
Artist: Paul Elliman

Unlike the painter who can say 'This particular painting is not ready for the exhibition', you've got to be there at the first performance with something finished. This seems to be a pressure that suits you.

RB: It's a pressure that I often feel I can't deal with, but it's actually the one that I need to finish a piece, and that is quite terrifying for me. But I enjoy the risk. I enjoy the notion of the unexpected. Every day brings in another element that has to be solved, and there is also a responsibility to finish a piece in order to move on – in order to get rid of it – which is quite exciting. You have to allow a work to stay with you for so long and then let it go and try not to let it interfere with something new. There is a question of making it special and letting it go which I think is something which could be associated with other sorts of relationships.

How much – if at all – do you actually amend pieces?

RB: Never. I adapt them to fit with or respond to the space but that is part of the performance process. I don't amend the finished choreographic work.

Not at all? Once they're done they're done?

RB: Yes, because of that decision: 'On the day it's done, it's done'. That was the point that I decided to stop.

I've seen works which people take on tour and their attitude

is that by the last night of the tour the piece will be finished. I always think: 'What did the people who came on the first night get?'

RB: I can't do that. I'd rather cut it short in order to get it out than allow it to evolve.

You're saying that it's not just a question of accumulation. It's not just a question of the thing getting bigger and better. There's a lot of editing back that's required as well – a lot of throwing away – and that's always very difficult when you've worked on something for a while and you think that you've nearly got it there. Maybe the dancers are enthusiastic about it and you know it's not right.

RB: I think when you are dealing with the elements of improvisation and the demand of a performance you cannot be anything but caring about the nature of how you deal with what you're going to throw away. It's a very careful thing. I try to explain to the dancers that they're coming up with an overall concept that does not belong to anyone's individuality. Part of what they're creating will be in the finished work but in very different forms. Everything is valuable.

All that's from teaching – that's why I don't deny all those years of teaching in schools and colleges. The work with very young children, for instance, was all about spontaneity and imagination. It was communication on a very fast level between me and all those young people. It's relevant to the way my work is processed. It's about the immediate seeing and understanding of the moment – the eye and the moment and the mood.

In the end I probably only use very little of what's done in the studio. If as a dancer you make a lot of material, then you've got more chance of performing some of it. On the other hand, sometimes somebody can do very little and it becomes totally significant. I don't think you can do anything about that. I think dancers have to live with that. That's why they are special people. They have to live with the idea that the process is selective and it is a selection that rests with someone else. I'm careful with that.

While you've done some work for 'alternative' spaces, spaces which are for something else, it's not been a constant thread has it?

RB: No, I'm not a site-specific person. I've done some works outside because it was a particular use of a particular space. I thought I was quite into it – but it could have been anywhere.

But you have worked in galleries a lot.

RB: I've worked in galleries because of the nature of the work. I think that the work is better when intimately viewed.

I think there is something about your work that requires an intensity of gaze which is very different to watching something happening in a proscenium or any kind of theatre setting.

RB: Occasionally I have sometimes been criticised for the lack of physicality, but I think that could be an interpretation based on the work being viewed from a distance. But it isn't actually true. The work is about the sense of the timing and the intention of what's going to happen. From a distance, that information is completely unconnected. You can gaze at it and say, 'Oh they're just moving around,' but there is a physical reason for everything, which needs to be seen.

That's similar to the difference between how you attend to a computer screen and a television screen. You sit back to look at a television screen and you lean forward to look at a computer screen. It requires a different kind of attention.

I also think that dance which appears on a proscenium carries with it the implications of theatre, narrative, characterisation. I think your work is first cousin to the visual arts, which for our generation are allusive, suggestive, to do with real, physical things.

Image as Event
BODY AS SITE 1993
Artist: Paul Elliman

Image as Event
BODY AS SITE 1993
Artist: Paul Elliman

N° 25

Body as Site
(All of these)

Tension and Compression
BODY AS SITE 1993, Artist: John Lyall

REFLECTIONS ON THE MAKING PROCESSES, 2001-2002

ROSEMARY BUTCHER and NIKI POLLARD,
with SUSAN MELROSE

The following observations, many of which were gathered over the two-year period, 2001-2002, but some of which come later, weave together a number of voices, a number of *times (before, in process, once more, after, again)*, a number of interventions and reflections on the making processes. Certain observations come from Niki Pollard's rehearsal-process observations, and respond directly to what she has seen there. Others attempt to catch at Rosemary Butcher's ongoing reflections on the new work - which is dynamic, ongoing; a new unfolding, where changing perceptions and ways of seeing[1] intersect with established patterns of work.

In repose, long enough to be seen by a public, each new piece of work embodies an unfinished, momentary manifestation of an ongoing process of reflection and questioning. The staging seen by the public, at any moment in time, at any site, figures as a single unfolding, which never quite realises the philosophical enquiry which moves it. Thought (as action) - critical, interrogative, speculative - continues, over years, marked, punctually, by external factors which press in on it. What might be the most striking, to some readers, with regard to the artist's thought processes and reflections, is the fact that 'the work' surprises its maker, once 'it' emerges, and begins to stabilise itself. Her enquiry, and her speculation, continues, long after the show has emerged, and after it has been seen by an audience. Hence her own 'knowledge-status', as performance-maker, with regard to 'the work', remains tentative, hesitant, questioning, bemused - even anxious; and it seems appropriate to observe that it is something unresolved, in the previous work or works, which will inform another undertaking.

Wherever the font changes, below, so too did the time of reflection, the observer, as well as the position from which the observation is made. In this chapter, we seek to articulate something of the weave of thought-as-choreographic-action with which this book has sought to engage. Wherever passages are marked 'RB', these are the most intimate reflections on the work in question. At the same time, it should be noted that we are asking the impossible here: that 'the visual artist' *speak her practice* - which, as choreographer/philosopher she has systematically preferred not to.

1. *SCAN*: instruction, reflection, perception

Think about holding the skeleton, holding onto it wherever it is in the body, onto whatever is holding you up. Hold up your own body and another's. Drop.

RB: *SCAN* **came from trying to look outside and inside of the body, at the bright and dark extremes of radiographic images. The lighting provides not illumination so much as sensation, screening the body. I did not want things to be wholly seen.**

X-ray made it possible to look non-invasively inside a human body and illuminate skeletal and tissue structures. In *SCAN,* movement becomes radiographic, exposing attenuated images of the body that are as startling as for the first time seeing one's X-ray image.

When you move a bone, know how that holds up your skeleton so that your partner can reinforce it. If you see a place where you can hold, lift the body up. Grab with a hold. Layer, press down. You haven't got time to think. Come at it with three different options. Out of the relation of grabbing, you both fall. Break out the energy.

Manipulating their own and one another's limbs, the dancers are as if oblivious to their own mindful existence. Any emotional resonance appears accidental and residual to the everyday-body - a head is turned aside to avoid being struck in the face by a partner's fast-swinging arms; a lack of eye-contact appears as one dancer grabs another to her or his feet with his hands clamped over her cheek-bones. *SCAN* is saturated with these apparently 'accidental' moments.

J. Harvey, writing about 'Movement in Fiction', noted in the late 1990s that '[t]he movement of human consciousness in crisis is a vast, slow rushing... [P]erception itself races so events seem to drag. We are at once at the quick, and at the slow, of human awareness.'[2] *SCAN* reveals the 'quick' of human awareness in dense, impacted detail as a relentless 'vast slow rushing'. But in *SCAN*, in addition, is there a 'movement of human consciousness in crisis'? Certainly whatever has triggered it is not brought to a climax, not resolved in the work, even in the time of the event, which reaches its end. *SCAN* takes us, jolts us - and then leaves us there.

Movement is thrust into brief, razor-edge junctures. Surges of taut energy ricochet out and seem to peel away the sides of the dancer's bodyspace. Migrating across the space in a tightly knotted square, the internal angles of duets continually realign. In a single moment, a torso is sucked backwards with tensile energy, an arm whipped out and a brittle body falls across another's pathway.

Take wading, presenting and grabbing. Then wade, present, grab. No movement finishes, but it finds a way to resolve. The operating control is from behind. Work on squares of possibility. Look for ways for the movement to keep going, flying with a slightly controlled element. Push bones into space and into each other. Pulse backwards.

RB: I wanted to do away with the superfluity that was solely choreographic craft and reveal instead sensorial images of the body in a dense, pixellated work. Yet, in the end, I realised that the dance form was still embedded in the movement.

There is suspension and grounding in the wading. Trying to stay afloat by treading water, and a body grounded, activated by another rather than active in itself.

Rosemary Butcher cites Bill Viola's *The Messenger* as an influence in the making of *SCAN*: in the Viola piece a submerged figure is seen indistinctly rising to the surface to inhale, then sinks away with agonising slowness. Viola describes treating visual images as if, like sound, they can penetrate the perceiving body[3] and find 'a resonant frequency latent in all spaces... a vital link between the unseen and the seen.'[4]

RB: *SCAN* **is crammed with visual holes.**

Viewed from four sides, movement appears to be interlocked and overlain so as to be only ever partially seen from each viewing position. Slit white lighting states and momentary blackouts cut further gaps i n the visible fabric.

Diminish the whole by finding the central peak of the material. Everything can decrease, become sparse, but no one can leave the space.

RB: Visually, my concern was for what I wanted to be remembered of material that flickers continuously with bursts of energy. In a way, everything is seen, but some moments are more geared up to be memorable. Little is wasted; I had to be exacting to duplicate sensation without repeating movement material.

Increasingly, things that do not stop appear. Find ways to fly over. Lifts are always going somewhere. In a suspension, the floor has parted company with your feet leaving you hanging.

Find ways for the lifts to exist only in time, like stillness. Take that information and refer it back to your body.

RB: The double duet structure was the solution to a mechanical problem of having a sense of floating or of being submerged without the buoyancy of water. I could only use the vertical due to the spatial confinement. The doubled-up nature of two sets of duets creates flickering energies in the space.

Risk the balance and fall in two planes.

A dancer repeatedly shunts her partner into the air so that he is seen momentarily in flight, his hands hooked and oddly rigid like a flailing boxer. The image hangs in fractional stasis like the mid-explosion debris of Cornelia Parker's *Cold, Dark Matter, An Exploded View*. Eerily, hiatus in *SCAN* seems to be reached as much by hovering energy as by the frantic, pulsed sections. Both crammed and holed states are held, seemingly interminably, as if the work slips and then breaks between parallel worlds. In one, bodies flicker incessantly; in the other, they hang in free fall.

Stretch open the chest cavity, string the bones differently. Cover and flush. Keep the image going. Flush.

RB: No one is self-sufficient; *SCAN's* **density makes it baroque and choral.**

Split. Then drop. No preparation, just suspend and drop.
Let the weight fall from under you. Go back into it
straightaway.

RB: Movement was phased to avoid climaxes; 'grabbing' had
urgency, a sense of dropping, 'to present' was architectural.
The main thing was pace, intricacy, sensation; keeping it going
with decisions made on the spur of the movement. I did not know
what I had. The question was rather of whether I could sustain it.
I searched for ways in which the piece could hover after the flurry
of the first ten minutes and then topple over, fall off the edge a
little. Tip over into something bigger than itself just at the moment
when it becomes overwhelmed. The eye cannot take in everything.

Grabbing — holding — leaning — pressing — falling from
holding on.

The visual plane seems to tilt, with the expanding angle of a dancer's
arm as he tips his partner precariously away from the vertical. No visible
support prevents her falling from the ledge of his spine. Time, too,
seems to skew as live, present activity reverses into filmed images
from rehearsal. Close-up images of a hand flick into sight from darkness,
cup light and drop away. In Grotowski's resonant early writing on
performance, 'impulse and action are concurrent: the body vanishes,
burns, and the spectator sees only a series of visible impulses'.[5]

RB: In letting go of a front, I let go of control over how it will be
seen. The film gives a completely different viewpoint that does
not interfere. It was Vong's decision to project film into the space
left by the dancers, introducing documentary, trace-like qualities.
It makes SCAN be not about just one thing although it picks out
one person's view. At the end of the film, I ask myself: 'What have
I seen?'

In the film, projected dance movement unravels disconcertingly into
hesitant sketches and inconsequential gestures, excised in rehearsal
from the live performance. They provide a pre-performance imagery,
ghosting it. By including rehearsal footage, Vong frames live performance
reflectively, as provisional endpoint. Perhaps it is, in Bruce Nauman's
phrase, so he can 'keep taking it apart', admit of no final version.[6]

Adopting documentary strategies, the film disarmingly recalls certain
preceding moments of the live performance, offering an ironic 'behind
the scenes' insight. Shots of Rosemary's feet, hands and clavicle
appear, beginning a tentative portrait of the choreographer dissected,
just as one becomes aware that perception of the work overall
is fragmented. The film freezes as Butcher's face is turned to the
camera: what does she see? A 'never-ending flicker between three
interchangeable figures' begins, and 'audience, choreographer and
dancers are at once subject and object'.[7]

By representing Butcher in the process of making the piece that is
being watched, the film locks SCAN into constitutive ambiguity. It forces
us to ask unanswerable questions: what does Rosemary Butcher see
- what is she looking at? Perhaps spectators themselves are chasing
something here, trying to see too far back, turning to see what is
already lost, because it has been lost? SCAN, too densely framed to
be held by the eye, is - as Jorie Graham might write - 'disappearing
into the seen'.[8]

Present a bone and pass it through your body. Take one
and transfer it somewhere else, then throw it away.

RB: Much of the piece is unaccountable to me. I do not know how
I made those decisions, although they seemed absolutely right at
the time. Like any piece, it is made up of a lot of mistakes and
the decisions you forced because you could not get to where
you wanted by any other means. A notion of a purity of making
is mistaken. I allowed some things to be as there were enough
of the things I wanted. If I wanted to keep a second instant, I had
to keep the first even though I might not be able to account for
why it was there. I was constantly questioning whether something
should go or stay, but the fact of keeping it moving was more
important than where it moved.

Wash your bones. Present the ribs, the front and back
of the body. Build it up, bringing it out into the
space, adding dimension and tension. Simplify the bone
moving so that is more operated and agitated. Keep going
— you are going to split the energy so that it becomes
less symmetrical.

Keep going...

BODY AS SITE
Prep work at the Holborn Centre 1992

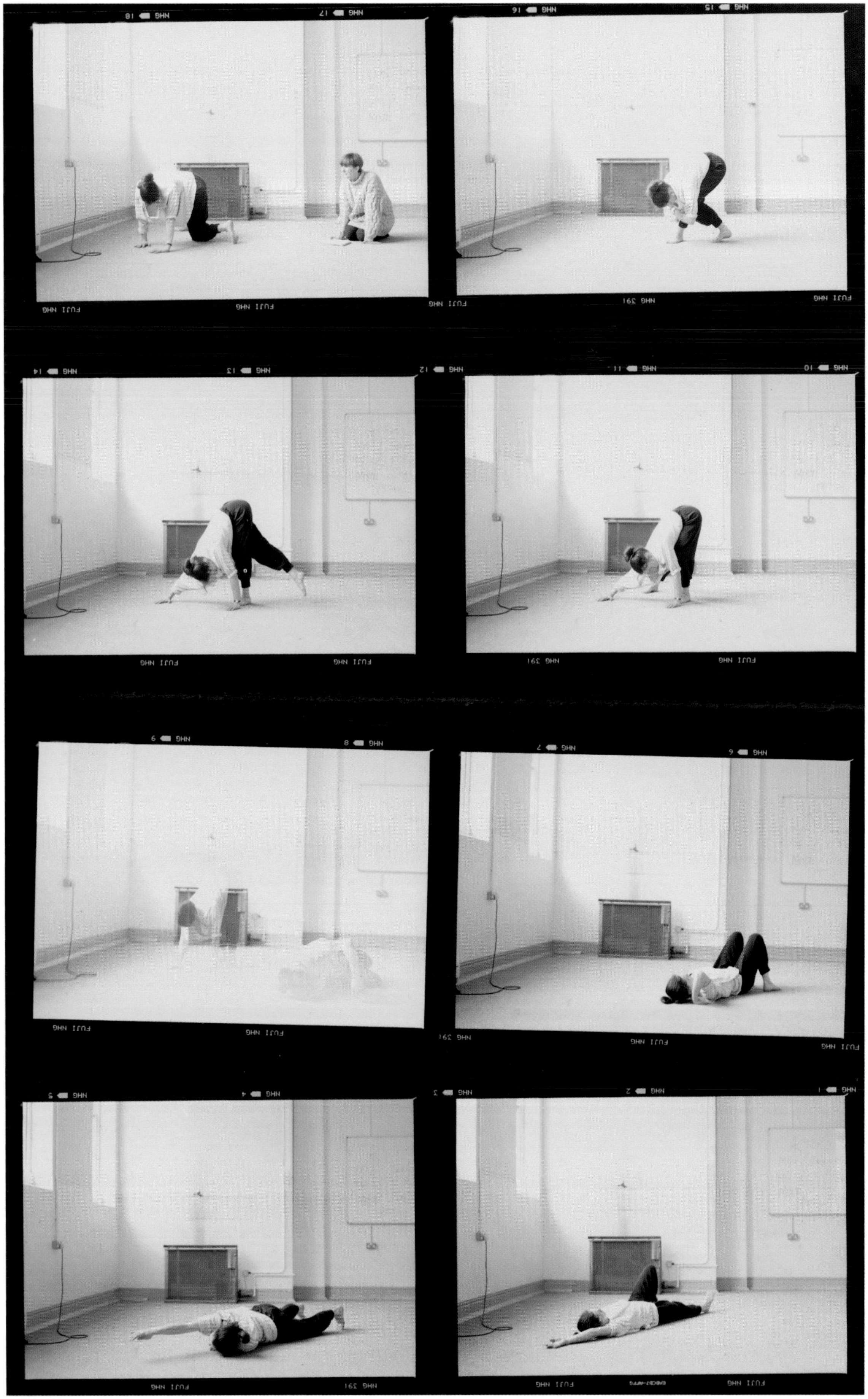

2. Falling upwards: in rehearsal for *Three Views from Vertical,*

August 2001

'O it has vibrancy, she thought, this emptiness, this intake just prior to the start like a sickness this wanting to snag, catch hold, begin'.
(Jorie Graham) [9]

'Finding holes, that is what interests me'.
(Rosemarie Tröckel) [10]

Where does new work come from? How does the artist keep on growing - since she must? Rosemary Butcher quotes Rosemarie Tröckel's words, having seen her video work, *Sleeping Pill*, at the 1999 Venice Biennale: 'finding holes, that is what interests me'. Ideas for a new work seem to surface even as *SCAN* is previewed, suggesting that the creative research and development activity - the epistemic, [11] as well as the creative - continues, independently of the programme of public viewing. The production is revealed as momentary, a pause in an ongoing unfolding of 'something', a momentary realisation which is non-identical with what drives it.

Butcher speaks of holes as 'an absence of presence' and as 'a moment not yet present, not yet turned on', and recalls Gogol's phrase, 'without even leaving, we are no longer there.' [12] The improvisation tasks - launch, veer and brace for landing - all sourced from a paragliding guide (*Field Events*), seem however to demand that the performers be thoroughly present in the rehearsal material-real. They are both real, present, and symbols, emerging metaphor. The request comes that the performers Charles Linehan and Rahel Vonmoos start with a functional pedestrianism, 'from where it has no extras', and must deal, then, with the immediate reality 'of your body preparing itself to fall'. While concentrated on the embodied moment, meanwhile, they seem to an observer's eye oddly 'not yet turned on' - as if they wait, held in a state of non-arrival, not comprehending detail, but grasping the larger quest, as quest.

The earliest instructions are to consider the notions of *launch, veer and brace*, while working with positions adopted in paragliding, aware that the body is held while in motion: 'Think of places where your body is in one place but really doing something else'. With their attention directed to a physically internalised alertness, a dynamic field of activity, Butcher observes out loud that they look as if they are 'planning, not dancing'. Planning is head-centred, dancing is feet. What is seen, however, might also be mistaken, in the words we struggle to bring to it. Words can invent what seems to be seen, but may actually point elsewhere...

The strategy of 'finding holes' through the performers' focus on a reality differently experienced to that seen (because the dancer never quite sees what we others see), creates a process and an attitude, where movement seems encrypted, to mean more than it is doing. In rehearsal, Butcher approaches the performers' material as an already-existing code to be cracked: 'When you are in M, is that a possible code for a parachute? I need to note down the possible eventualities.' Emerson wrote that every natural fact is a symbol of some spiritual reality. Certainly Butcher seems to be trying to decipher a real, where physical events, perceived, serve as symbolic types, scrutinised for evidence that salvation might come.

Paradoxically, even as she works on decoding the performers' movement, which they give her less or more attentively, she seems drawn to the notion of the indecipherable in the memory of each of us. In one of her process notebooks a comment attributed to Bill Viola is recorded: 'Memory is the residing place of life-experience, the collection that reveals and/or fabricates order and meaning.' One improvisation instruction, then, is to 'think of something reminiscent that you experience as real. It is a literal fall. I am redirecting that energy into the abstract. You are constantly reminded of the other place.'

Rosemary asks the performers to remember 'everything', layering those memories into their movements - so that they provide sites to be moved across, in place of clearly defined actions or temporal sequences (such as we find in narrative dance). Her words, spoken to the performers, mark these sites progressively, but inevitably there is too much, and much of the precise detail of what is experienced is forgotten. Selected, sited, reproduced, rehearsed movement, coded and layered by misplaced reminiscences, becomes more and more inscrutable. The choreographic choices by which the performers treat their movement - loop, skip, 'scratch', amplify, diminish, compound - accentuating the fragmentary fabrication of memory. Emerson recognised that every man's condition is the solution, in hieroglyphic, to the enquiries he would put.

Slips and skips of memory do not seem adequate as a means to account for a condition arising in the work-in-progress that Butcher identifies: 'You are left with circumstances', she observes. 'No resolution, no eventuality.' No failure is involved, but the performer is struck by gradual loss, and the fear 'of multiplying useless gestures'. [13] Rosemary's choreographic field is similar to that of implacable memory, as it is described in Borges: 'in a field situation, each thing is the centre'. In this new work, as 'in the teeming world of Funes' there are 'only details, almost immediate in their presence'. [14]

The work's title, *Three Views from Vertical*, suggests a geometric and geographic attention to circumstantial and unresolved topographical qualities which are at play when Butcher speaks of a form in which 'events are contained in an installation, not passing through time'. In rehearsal, she asks the performers for seemingly endless, levelled-out states in which they 'disband their normal sense of time so that it has to be watched until the last moment.' Butcher cites Paul Virilio, echoing this shifted sense of duration, observing the 'emergence of a new concept of time, which is no longer exclusively the time of classic chronological succession, but now a time of (chronoscopic) exposure of the duration of events at the speed of light'. [15] 'Would you never be ready to move on?' Butcher asks the performers.

Curiously, when Butcher speaks of her works, their interrelations also appear structured by Virilio's notion of exposure, rather than by notions of succession. In her accounts, ideas thread between works as if through wormholes, revealing the larger, ongoing research project and philosophical enquiry. For example, Rosemary says of *SCAN* that 'the fact of keeping it moving was more important than where it moved' yet, 'in the end, I realised that the dance form was still embedded in the movement.' Her comment mirrors another in an interview on *Flying Lines* the previous year: 'I seemed to be more concerned with ongoing energy than I did with exactness. In some ways it is a pedestrian piece that comes out as a pure dance piece'. [16]

In *Three Views from Vertical*, she is again preoccupied with work that, while choreographic, is not necessarily dance - hence her interest in

Tröckel, whom she sees as a video artist working choreographically. In the *Flying Lines* interview, she describes a discarded idea of plummeting falls, prompted by her recall of Tröckel's *Sleeping Pill*. This is not inter'textual' – rather, it is an example of interpractice; and to the extent that it further articulates the ongoing enquiry into arts practices, it is interpraxiological, a critical enquiry into practice *through* creative practice.

John Hall in the poem 'Meaning Insomnia' observes that words 'in an appalling irresolution of undisclosed destiny need their sleep'.[17] Something similar might be true of movement, in Butcher's enquiry, unresolved and exposed, since 'sleeping naturally happens when you are dealing with time'. Sleeping is felt as a diurnal hole in the experience of daily continuum; the lack of consciousness experienced as an 'absence of presence.' Creating conditions for sleeping - the premise for Tröckel's *Sleeping Pill* - thus also creates the conditions for 'finding holes', strewing gaps, fragments, openings, *breaks*.

Butcher describes these gaps and breaks not only as non-arrival, but as 'points at which you make a decision' - like a climber's fractional pause, after reaching out to, but before clasping, a handhold. Almost invisibly, in *Three Views from Vertical,* breaks where decisions take hold radiate and punctuate energies, with a spectator in mind.

Viewed from without, this choreographic mending of the visible[18] creates a correspondence between strategies for 'finding holes', and those that treat movement as circumstantial event. The practical and geometric rigour of Butcher's ideas of flight and falling resonate in her approach with a blunt comment of Le Corbusier: 'The lesson of the airplane lies in the logic which governed the statement of the problem and its realisation'.[19] In finding holes through launch and flight, she opens up a reverse vertigo. In Virilio's words:

> The breakaway of the Wright brothers on their first take-off from the beach at Kitty Hawk, show[s] us another way, an exotic reorganisation of sight that would finally take account of a possible fall upwards, from now on our sky is vanishing.[20]

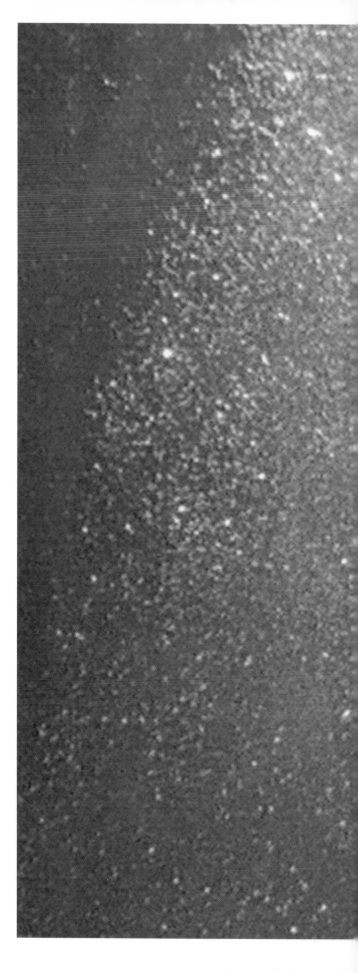

3.
*Undercurrent
(for Cathy
Greenhalgh)
and Three
Views From
the Vertical*

2001

In 2001, Rosemary Butcher made a new performance work, but also choreographed a short film, directed and performed by Cathy Greenhalgh, entitled *undercurrent*. The two are linked, in the sense that they together represent two unfoldings - two momentary instantiations - of a single contemplative and speculative engagement, which continues beyond them. The film's movement material comes from two activities: jumping on a trampoline and plunging into a swimming pool. The central task is to choreograph movement that is not grounded, but sinking through water or falling through air.

The trampoline takes over from human contact with the ground: it lifts the performer into the air, without wings, and the air embraces her as she falls. The performer is *not quite flying*; *not quite here but not quite gone*; *not quite in the air, and then she is back*. Her state is a *state-between*, which choreography seeks to capture, and to pass on. As long as that state is almost ungrounded, it seems to us to lean toward the philosophical, which a spectator might grasp, as though in a flash of recognition:

RB: The water and trampoline were both what I call 'interventions'. Their impact upon the movement was not caused by a human decision, but by the nature of something else happening. As an example, the film has underwater shots of the haze of bubbles created by the impact of a body plunging into water. The bubbles intervene in how movement is seen, and are a consequence of working in water that is out of the performer's control.

For the immersed shots, we were concentrating on practical tasks of suspension, floating and the impact of falling into water. For the trampoline shots, we dealt with directly coming into and leaving a space. In live performance, such directness is impossible as one cannot, without transition, 'get rid' of anybody from the performance space.

What became apparent as soon as the rushes were made was an emerging sensuality of images of the body in water and in air. With *undercurrent,* we are close to the vulnerability of a suspended body, to a sense of almost nothing going on.

This sort of intervention similarly operated in *Three Views from Vertical*:[21]

RB: At the start of the project, I was thinking about World War II images of bomber formations and parachute drops, and imagined intervention in terms of things falling from the sky. I was interested in Rosemary Tröckel's *Sleeping Pill* (Venice Biennale, 1999). I worked awhile with an image of performers suspended, a short distance from the ground, in suits of some kind, out of which they could be dropped at irregular intervals. Another early design idea was that some performers would provide a constant falling from height, a plane of activity somehow walled off from that of the other performers.

The design plans in this instance, however, no longer include an architectural structure to fall from:

RB: I was beginning to think as much of flight as of falling, of runways, aerial formation, gliding and flight paths. The action of falling from height was transferred into the horizontal plane, becoming movement along the diagonals that we called 'low flying'. Rather than high falling, I began to think of the performers as always coming forwards, as if along a runway. I became more

concerned too with journeying to an edge, with the activity of climbing and resting on ledges, before inevitable falling.

Three Views from Vertical has to do with episodes of time, with an idea of light moving and of darkness. I recently came upon the work of Sophie Ricketts who photographs night scenes. I am interested in how she might set up a performance space for photography, perhaps with just a tiny thread of light and darkness all around.

As in the films of Tacita Dean, I want to make work that is more connected with what is apparent; with what is going on but not put into a space simply to fill it, to make up an event. This is the nature of *undercurrent*; while seeing the same things, we are conscious of the phasing of time, impact and fall-off. For *Three Views from Vertical,* I have worked with the performers on trying to break down the dance element of their movement and work with actual sensations, to weave between 'abstract' and 'real'. In the physical predicaments arising from our studio improvisations and in the preoccupations of their lives, I have been asking them to be concerned with ideas of risk and rescue, fall and survival.

Three Views from Vertical premiered in September 2001. After recent works for installation and gallery settings, it took place on a proscenium arch stage, which brought with it its own constraints, its own possibilities, its own expectations:

RB: The new piece is in an odd place structurally. I do not have studio time with the dancers until August. Looking at video footage from rehearsals, I can see that the material is too intricate to create the runway image in the large, distanced space of the Vienna stage. What I think I have done too is to combine material from one idea and put it into another, where it cannot rest. The detailing of the existing movement is so exact that I may have to start again with different material. I probably need to leave the runway idea and cut the material down to something that can be intimate within the scale of the Vienna stage.

I worry about the intimacy of the movement and about how difficult it is choreographically to sustain image. I find I have a love-hate relationship with work that I am making. What I am beginning to think more and more is that in order for the piece to survive, I must magnify what is happening and juxtapose scale. The only way the runway image might work would be with a moving light beam but I don't want the structural problem to be resolved through design. Increasingly, I find that my choreographic decisions are not restricted to the movement.

My struggle is to resist the momentum towards the piece existing solely as dance performance. Elements other than human movement are needed; an environment, something that intervenes and is outside of the performers. A moving light, like a lighthouse beam, might intervene, for example, picking up movement as it tracks across the stage. Events are going on, but only some are seen before going into darkness. I have not yet found the context, the angle of the movement. The nearest I have come is with this idea of another environment, of light that keeps coming round cutting them into and out of darkness.

The detail and intimacy of the existing material seem at first sight not to allow an environment to intervene in the performers' activity.

RB: I love the 'realness' in what the performers are doing, the juxtaposition of figures. *SCAN* had proximity; the new piece must deal with distance. The detailing of the movement needs to happen - but at a distance. Yet if I do not solve the detailing, all that will be seen will be performers seeming to pitch around.

What I think I have come back to is the concept of real time that I was trying to deal with all along. Earlier today, I was watching video footage showing a task I set the dancers of re-working duet structures without their partner. How they responded has the strange quality of 'realness' that I am seeking; what they are doing becomes about the absence of the thing it was made with.

The new piece has gone through a number of different titles: *Weaving the Rainbow; Cloudbase; Field Events; Three Views from Vertical…* Each emphasises space, human perception, and natural processes:

RB: It is now called *Still-Slow-Divided* for the British premiere in Birmingham, February 2002. I have made certain changes and cast shifts since the performance of what was then *Three Views from Vertical* in Vienna.

Due to production costs, we would not have been able to achieve the ideas that I then had in mind, of a tracking, thin strip of light and a wipe-out brightening. I had thought that all the movement would take place within one space, but later shifted the structure to two lit squares. The lighting designer, Anthony Bowne, suggested instead rigging a single film-light overhead in each square.

At times in the piece, I see those two spaces as two rooms highlighted in terms of danger, as in the section that I call 'the conversation' where the two figures in the front space are to me as intelligence officers decrypting enemy transmissions during World War II.

At only one fulcrum moment, Deborah Jones runs the length of a diagonal, bringing the two parallel spaces into a two-way spatial relation that changes the nature of the piece.

There is a pure, solitary light, slightly menacing within the context of the performance.

RB: I think of an aircraft's landing lights coming down through a night sky, and inversely, on the ground, of a landing strip lighting up to the sky. Overhead lighting gives an edge to the movement so that, in spite of the proscenium arch separation from the audience, its detail is never lost.

The work changes after Rosemary sees it performed in Vienna. This dynamism suggests that her interventions, at any one time, remain speculative, despite the momentary material instantiation which is 'the show' - even beyond the moment, then, when the work is viewed in public.

RB: The piece now has the environment provided by Cathy Lane's sound-score and Anthony Bowne's lighting design. *Still-Slow-Divided* deals with the physicality of flying, both in the dancers' sense of their bodies and in the predicament of an individual. There is a 'humanness' to the dancers that is not at all about trying to take on an abstraction of parachuting. I think I can see now that the work is as much to do with people on the ground, and indeed with people on the ground who might be flying. I had in mind wartime footage of night parachute drops over enemy territory; thousands of figures falling silently from looming aircraft.

The 'rescues' - moments of almost stilled contact between two figures - remind the onlooker of people who have landed but are escaping. Some aspects of the piece work straightforwardly with the thematics of danger and survival.

RB: Survival is a matter of being on the edge and recovering. Initially, I had not intended to deal in this work with the human content that comes when partner-work is used. While I cannot fully explain how my decisions were made, brief moments of contact did come back into the piece after September 11th.

Still-Slow-Divided works with moments in time, with task and obstacle; being on the edge and abseiling down, climbing with a partner and falling. I began to try and isolate what I felt were moments of the 'real' from the dancers' movement, moments so accurately perceived by the dancer that the movement becomes highly particular. For example, Rahel Vonmoos' parachute fall of her legs tipping over, and of how she manoeuvres within a visualised parachute harness. In a way it all goes back to the vertical and horizontal, to that idea of leaning over the edge, flying and landing.

Rolling and falling also came from the idea of crossing an assault course with an instructor. The dancers worked in partners, one shouting orders to the other for negotiating the imagined obstacles. Always, falling is the thing inevitable after climbing; the relationship between vertical and horizontal.

Cathy Lane makes a new sound score for the piece - one final element to come to the work before the performance in Vienna:

RB: I had asked Cathy Lane to start partly from sound that would be reminiscent of the experience of flying a World War II bomber, or of being on the ground in expectation of an air-raid; sounds of sirens, of radio and morse code transmissions, of aircraft engines heard from the cabin. In one section of the score, Cathy used the sound of a squeaky farm gate and of wood pigeons suggesting to me a nervous expectancy of the summer of 1942.

Certain sounds have contemporary resonance, like the insistent ringing of mobile phones that needle the hearer as to why the call is not answered. Through the final phases of *Still-Slow-Divided*, the sound score increases in density to overpower the performers. As tension builds climactically towards an inevitability of disaster, the movement events contract to the more and more residual. To me, Cathy's score accentuates the quality of danger and anticipation in *Still-Slow-Divided,* a final layer of information on the sense I sought of the 'real'.

Endnotes

1   The term is from John Berger, from his text of the same name, *Ways of Seeing*, Penguin, 1972. It has 'gone into the language'.

2   J. Harvey, 'Movement in Fiction', *Introduction to Contemporary Fiction Since 1970*, (ed. R. Mengham), Cambridge: Polity Press, 1999: 83

3   Ibid.

4   Ibid.

5   Grotowski, Jerzy *Towards a Poor Theatre*, Barba, Eugenio (ed.) London: Methuen, 1969 [no page reference]

6   Nauman, Bruce, cited by Van Bruggen

7   M. Foucault, cited by I.Hedges in *Breaking the Frame*, Indianapolis: Indiana University Press, 1991.

8   Jorie Graham, 'Orpheus and Eurydice', *The Dream of the Unified Field, Selected Poems, 1974-94*, Manchester: Carcanet, 1996

9   Jorie Graham, 'Vertigo', *ibid*. p.64

10 Attributed to Rosemarie Tröckel by Rosemary Butcher in conversation.

11 'Epistemics' refers to any 'knowledge-centred' activity, and to the models of intelligibility brought to bear on the objectives sought. One such model is 'the rehearsal'; a second is 'the show itself', and the production values which inform it.

12 Gogol, quoted in P. Virilio, *Open Sky*, London: Verso, 1997, p.3

13 Jorge Luis Borges, 'Funes the Memorious', *Labyrinths*, Penguin, London, 1962, pp.87-95 (p.94)

14 Borges, p.94

15 Virilio, p.3

16 The pedestrian is most fully theorised by Michel de Certeau, writing in the late 1970s, whose *Practice of Everyday Life* appears in English translation by Steven Rendall, University of California Press, Berkeley, Los Angeles and London, in 1984.

17 John Hall, 'Meaning Insomnia', *A Various Art,* (ed. Andrew Crozier, Tim Longville), Paladin Poetry, London, 1990, p.133

18 Graham, p.36

19 Le Corbusier

20 Virilio, p.2

21 *Three Views from Vertical* premiered in Vienna in September 2001. The piece was later presented in a UK premiere in Birmingham 2002 with an amended cast under the new title, *Still-Slow-Divided*.

STILL-SLOW-DIVIDED 2002

STILL-SLOW-DIVIDED 2002

STILL-SLOW-DIVIDED 2002

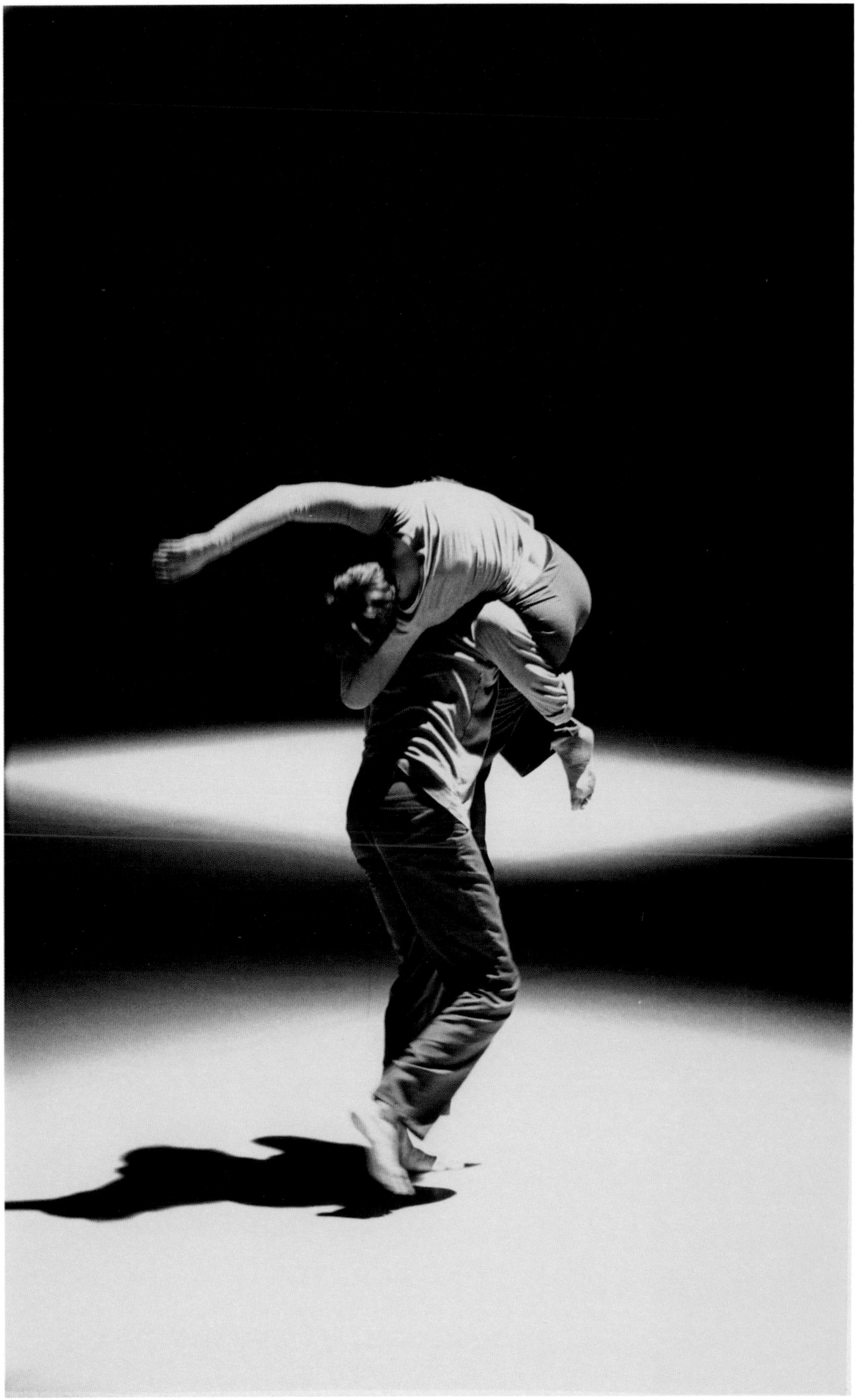

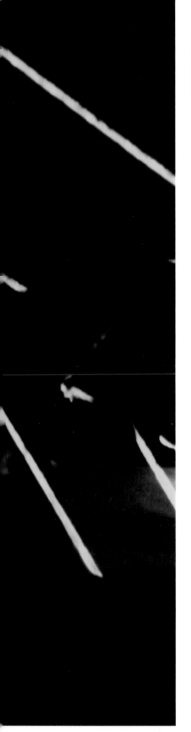

TRACES 1983

ROSEMARY BUTCHER: RETROSPECTIVE INSIGHTS, 1976-2001

JANET LANSDALE

PAUSE AND LOSS 1976

The retrospective of Rosemary Butcher's work at the Royal College of Art held early in October 1996 offered a reflective opportunity for those of us who had seen her work over a period of time as well as for new audiences. At that time, Rosemary Butcher had more than thirty-five works to her credit, many of them full-length collaborations lasting an hour or more. She had a studio named after her at the Holborn Centre for Performing Arts, and a chapter is devoted to her in a book of essays as one of a selected band of British choreographers.[1]

1. S. Jordan, *Striding out*, London: Dance Books, 1992

This retrospective of twenty years of creative exposition was both well-deserved and instructive in the terms of the history of our recent past. *Pause and Loss* and *Landings*, the subjects of the launch of the retrospective, were first performed at the Serpentine Gallery in March 1976, twenty-six years ago. They took the form of lunchtime concerts. Simple as this sounds today, it was in many ways a radical statement for its time, firstly in setting dance in an art gallery and secondly in the time of day – lunchtime dance concerts in art galleries were not a common occurrence then – nor are they now. Few of the Judson Dance Theatre's practices had filtered through from New York to England by that time.

It is necessary to ask how we see works of twenty-five years ago. What kind of insight do we bring compared to what a spectator in 1976 might have brought? Are such works in effect dead or alive for us? Is it too soon to revive postmodernism? Perhaps when its works can be 'exhumed' it is a sign that we can be said to have passed on to something else. But given postmodernism's interest in the past, this may not be the case – it is always revisiting its own and previous histories. Whether Rosemary Butcher owes a closer affiliation to modernism or postmodernism is itself a matter of debate and one that may be pursued through a reflection on her body of work. Jann Parry's reflections on an earlier series of reconstructions are illuminating. As she wrote, 'only if you let her create the mood and determine the pace… do you come away rewarded'[2] addressing common complaints of boredom or impatience at the almost hypnotic serenity of the work and the deliberately limited range of material.

2. J. Parry, 'Butcher alone', *The Observer*, May 25, 1986, p.19

A problematics of reconstruction of the works of Rosemary Butcher, as with any artist, has to expose subtleties in the different contexts, in the state of play of dance in 1976, 1986 and 1997, the years of the retrospectives, and now in 2003; the shifts in the artistic environment in which these works existed then and in which they are presented now; and the evolving purposes and processes of this artist and her performers. Articulating what it means to see the past through the eyes of the present is part of the challenge of new history. This paper particularly draws on works already reconstructed and those which were due to be completed before November 1997, i.e. from the middle period, *Spaces 4* (1981), *Traces* (1982), *The Site* (1983), *Imprints (*1983) and *Touch the Earth* (1987); and from the more recent period, *Body as Site* (1993), *After the Last Sky* (1995) and *Unbroken View* (1995). Through these events we were able to dwell on what remains constant, what is re-visited, and the complexity of our own positions as spectators and historians. I use the terms 'reconstructions' and 're-workings' advisedly, since these are revivals of pieces which were only ever partly set in the dance equivalent of tablets of stone (an odd notion for dance which points up its constant transience).

Some of these complexities can be revealed in the two revived works, *Pause and Loss* and *Landings*, where, for example, we see work which has been reconstructed in different ways, from a reworking of movement by different performers to exact reconstruction from video. In a sense, then, these are not the same works as those presented in 1976. Different individuals have re-interpreted the movement ideas, new dancers have observed the video movement and inflected their attempts at faithful revival in their own ways. In *Pause and Loss*, the dancers have the freedoms in performance that the original group had in 1976, working from its original starting points of shared phrases, chosen by the choreographer, to juxtapose, extend and play with fragments of material. The sensitivity of interplay – the dangers of performance – is partly what we are invited to consider. The discomfort for the dancers of not knowing what might happen is not inconsiderable and the problematic nature of terming this a 'reconstruction' is immediately evident.

Rosemary has commanded the respect, and indeed the continuing commitment in performance over lengthy periods of time of such well-established choreographers and dancers as Jonathan Burrows and Gill Clarke. The roll call of her dancers reads like a British new dance history: Maedée Duprès, Dennis Greenwood, Julyen Hamilton, Miranda Tufnell, Sue MacLennan, Yolande Snaith, Deborah Jones, Fin Walker, Kirsty Simpson, Russell Maliphant. In the 1996

PAUSE AND LOSS
Butlers Wharf, 1976

reconstructions we saw Jonathan Burrows, Gill Clarke, Dennis Greenwood, Henry Montes and Fin Walker. It is not convincing to suggest that these dancers/choreographers would be ciphers for previous dancers, aiming to re-create exactly what the first performers had done: rather they would, in important senses, 'construct' these works anew. Interestingly, Meisner[3] recalls being 'stunned' by *Body as Site* in 1993 and equally by the 1996-97 reconstruction, a clear indication, along with consistency of response among audiences and comment from other critics that, while performers may change, Rosemary Butcher's undying concerns remain visible.

Not least is the issue of identity of the work and ownership. The role of improvisation and the responsibilities of the dancers have been a continuing motif throughout Rosemary Butcher's work. Ramsay Burt conducted an interview with her in 1988 that exposed the contradictions of being both spontaneous and obsessed with form. In her terms, choreography is about 'finding a language through which you can allow other people to say what you want to say… it's allowing their body to say it in their sort of way'.[4] It is saying, however, what *Butcher* wants to say, albeit in the *dancer's* own way. And, as Burt points out, it is still 'saying something'. There is much more to be said about the often simplistic characterisation of Butcher's work as abstract minimalism in terms of its deeply humanistic subject matter and democracy of the treatment of the material.

Nonetheless, these two works give a flavour of Rosemary Butcher's concerns sustained through time. Such comments as her determination to continue with her own artistic vision, and her integrity in the face of a rapidly changing dance world, feature large in critics' reviews of her work over the period since 1976. Her unbending commitment has often been to her disadvantage in terms of obtaining funding and criticisms there have been, indeed, for the sustaining of a vision through time despite other developments in dance and the arts. Failing to respond to the vagaries of fashion, while officially respected, carries overtones of foolhardiness or blindness – it seems to me that 'artistic integrity' is a mixed blessing in a climate of reducing funding for the arts. As Sherril Dodds concluded in an article on Rosemary Butcher, her formalist concerns are not the current flavour. Dodds describes the working process thus: 'she peels away the layers of an idea, happily discarding piles of material, pushing her way through until she finds the purest of gems…

3. N. Meisner, 'Rosemary Butcher', *Dance Now*, 6 (2), 22-26, 1997

4. R. Burt, 'Finding a Language', *New Dance*, 44, Summer 1988, pp.12-14

her work feels like a breath of fresh air: simple, cerebral, serene'.[5]

Whether her vocabulary speaks significantly to human feelings or is simply too abstracted, too 'pure', too 'minimalist' for the late 1980s was a question for Jann Parry.[6] It carries a misleading assumption that we only need, or expect to have, one kind of art at a time; it is a view which fails to see that a multiplicity of art forms exist side by side, in various interesting relationships through time. Rarely does one end at the moment another starts. It can also be said that one reason so many forms exist simultaneously is that we need the richness of many kinds of work, appealing to different human sensibilities in distinctive ways. That Rosemary Butcher has sustained her view through changing art and cultural circumstances makes her vision and originality even more obvious.

Somewhat earlier, in 1987, Jann Parry had described Rosemary Butcher's new work at the time, *Touch the Earth*, as 'that rare thing, a completely satisfying fusion of dance, music and design'. In analysing this later twentieth-century version of collaboration, I am not sure that I would have used the term 'fusion' – with its high modernist overtones – but would prefer the terms in which Andrea Philips[7] describes Butcher's work as an 'athletic collision of art forms'. In some senses this is more meaningful.

When we think of collaboration in the twentieth century, we tend to bring to mind the extravaganzas of Diaghilev, the Brecht/Weill operatic visions, Martha Graham's intense total theatre or

5. S. Dodds, 'The momentum continues',
Dance Theatre Journal, 12 (X), 1997, pp.6-9

6. J. Parry *The Observer*,
Jan 29, 1989, p.46

LANDSCAPE
The Economist Building, London 1981

7. A. Phillips, 'The body as site', *Dance Theatre
Journal*, 10 (3), 1993, pp.50-52

Cunningham/Cage co-existence – all examples of similar processes, where cutting-edge artists of the time joined forces to create something greater than the sum of its parts. Yet these spectacular results were in a very different mode and mood from Rosemary Butcher's collaborative works. What they share, though, is this act of creation and of a sensuous world. This collaboration with architects, designers, composers, sculptors and film-makers is as important to her as it was to them.

Rosemary Butcher's work began by taking inspiration, for example, from Ben Nicholson's sculpture, and Paul Klee and Bridget Riley's paintings, but these influences soon gave way to collaborations with Dieter Pietsch, Jon Groom, John Lyall and Anya Gallacio. The diversity of these artists' backgrounds reveals the eclectic nature of her spatial vision and yet emphasises its centrality. Installations which provide a three-dimensional parallel to the moving body now inhabit the same space and participate directly in her work. Peter Noble's fabric and poles for *Flying Lines* (1985), for example, combined intimately with Michael Nyman's music, which, in this instance of a music-dance liaison, remained newly improvised in each performance. Collaborative constructions with such eminent artists are themselves both testimony to her position in the art world and to the equality of collaborative input.

Body as Site, made in 1993, and already re-visited in different physical 'sites', locates the debate firmly in dance, extending an invitation to look again at the body. Debates about subject and object can be located here. Collaborations with an architect, a designer, a composer and a composer-cum-sculptor, illuminate the performance ground. Her collaborators – Paul Elliman, Ron Haselden, John Lyall, Anya Gallacio and Simon Fisher-Turner – have received public recognition in their own right in the form of many awards, but yet they choose to join in this shared quest for an understanding of motion, or light and shade.

Locating Rosemary Butcher's work within the critical context of recent theorising in the arts, semiotic references abound, through signs and symbols associated with the visual arts and theatre, e.g. in *Traces* (1982) with its Paul Klee and Samuel Becket associations and in *Empty Signals* (1977). In a different vein, T.S. Eliot's *The Wasteland* provided a starting point for *After*

LANDSCAPE
The Economist Building, London 1981

the Crying and the Shouting (1989) which combined images of war-torn communities, more realistic subjects than are normally attributed to Rosemary Butcher.

Increasingly she has explored technological fantasies created by strips of light, by slide images or film loops playing simultaneously or with dancers in real time to bring another kind of motion into play and to question the prerogative of movement assumed by the dancing body. Other information, equally concerned with motion, but from different sources, is layered within and around this movement text. *Night Mooring Stones* (1984) created Scottish landscape sequences using four projectors for a film installation designed by Jill Rigby. These landscapes were commented upon by the dancers in movement, drawing attention to the contrast between spaces inside and outdoors, and to human interaction with different types of landscape through movement.

The works that Rosemary Butcher has created over twenty-five years can be characterised *in the art historical sense* as belonging to several 'periods', each revealing several thematic obsessions. Butcher herself loosely describes her works in the following way:

Battling with form	1974-1980	Twenty pieces over four years
Collaborations/the visual environment	1980-1987	Ten pieces over seven years
Expanding scale	1989-1992	Five pieces over four years
Returning to form	1993-1995	Four pieces over three years
Returning to the body	1996-2001	Three pieces over five years

This view of history, related as a chronology of event, in which early works give way to supposedly 'more mature' works, is not what is intended here. It would be one way of viewing history and thus of conceiving reconstruction, or creating the logic for a retrospective. But the chronology is less important than the sense that she focuses for a while on a group of inter-related issues and then moves on. Her works as a whole seem to share characteristics of the dances themselves; the ideas, like the movement, loop back and forth, they return in a new way to familiar ground,

PASSAGE NORTH EAST
Arnolfini Bristol 1976

they approach problems again and again but from yet another view. Her own imagery for *Flying Lines* (1985) might stand as a metaphor for a critical perspective, revealing the 'knotting, interlacing and veering off' images that stimulated it. Such language does not suggest a narrowly conceived logic or a linearity of historical progression.

These works tell many stories: works with titles such as *Traces* (1982) and *Imprints* (1983) evoke a sensibility which has the potential to move fluidly between emotional and structural pathways. In *Spaces 4* (1981), edges, boundaries and corners are challenged, while it is circles that are bisected in the 1982 solo *Field Beyond Maps*. The literal and the metaphoric rub shoulders in *Body as Site* where 'hieroglyphic catch phrases'[8] can be interpreted both literally as sign systems and less literally as archaeological traces of something that we never knew and can never have access to. In the first section of this work, this has its literal moments in the use of cats' eyes lining the floor, while in the final section, 'Recover', the apparently angelic creatures become 'icons without the trappings, purely structural angels [which yet] retain... their mystery'.[9]

8. Ibid. p.52

9. Ibid. p.52

Rosemary Butcher's work can be distinguished, then, from earlier collaborations and from co-existing new dance, in a number of significant respects – respects which indicate her alignment to postmodernist issues rather than to those of modernism. On the basis of her use of chance methods and improvisation, we can trace an affiliation with the Cage/Cunningham collaborations and other postmodernist works where the dancers' choices control the form of the work, if not its content. Through offering traces of many stories, and refusing a single, fixed narrative thread, we see how Rosemary Butcher, as Chris Crickmay long ago argued, sets up the 'conditions in which the dance may be found'; the post-structuralist emphasis on the role of the reader is thus exposed.[10]

10. C. Crickmay, 'Dialogues with Rosemary Butcher', *New Dance*, 36,1986, pp.10-13

By problematising the viewer and her position, and by creating works that take place in unusual spaces or outdoors (for example in *Passage North East* (1976)), or in more than one place simultaneously (as in *Multiple Event* (1976)), Rosemary Butcher challenges the viewer's notion that there is one 'dance' and that dance has a 'front' from which it is to be viewed.

PASSAGE NORTH EAST
Arnolfini Bristol 1976

PASSAGE NORTH EAST
Arnolfini Bristol 1976

In the creation of a dialogue that suggests to the long-term spectator the complexity of conversation and its multiple texts, she exposes threads that unravel or tighten, with fluidity, not a consistent drive to a climactic end. By overlapping and interweaving themes that dive and surface through the visual, musical and movement images, through the interaction of dancers among themselves, and with the material, she constructs an essay in imagery that speaks at many different levels. Applying this idea of creating many 'texts', extends the frame of references from literature to the fragments of the piece and their juxtaposition: in Rosemary Butcher's case, these 'texts' are of movement with a multiplicity of visual texts, together with sound, and literary or thematic, texts. Their very juxtaposition makes their relationship quite deliberately pointed and problematic – it is an intertextual relationship.[11]

This links to the idea of making visible the creative problems of the arts. For choreographers, this may involve revealing or exposing the process, for example, as Rosemary Butcher did in *Suggestion and Action* (1978), where instructions are called out to dancers, exposing analytic and construction processes. Questioning the fixity of the body is another indicator of a postmodernist sensibility, bringing to mind Foucault's notions of archaeology and feminist notions of 'writing the body' and its inscriptions. These concerns were pre-figured in *Imprints* (1983) with its notion of demolishing sites, and of pre-history. Work-a-day minimalism is one way of describing it, but glowing humanism and collaborative magic is another.

While writing the first version of this paper in 1996, I heard a talk on BBC Radio 3 by A.S. Byatt. Her discussion of Milan Kundera's *The Unbearable Lightness of Being* reminded me of a particularly apposite link which evokes some of the qualities of ambiguity that I find in Rosemary Butcher's work. Kundera[12] writes, 'the lightness/weight opposition is the most mysterious, most ambiguous of all'.

11. J. Adshead-Lansdale, (ed.), *Dancing texts: Intertextuality in interpretation,* London: Dance Books, 1999

12. M. Kundera, *The Unbearable Lightness of Being*, London: Faber, 1984

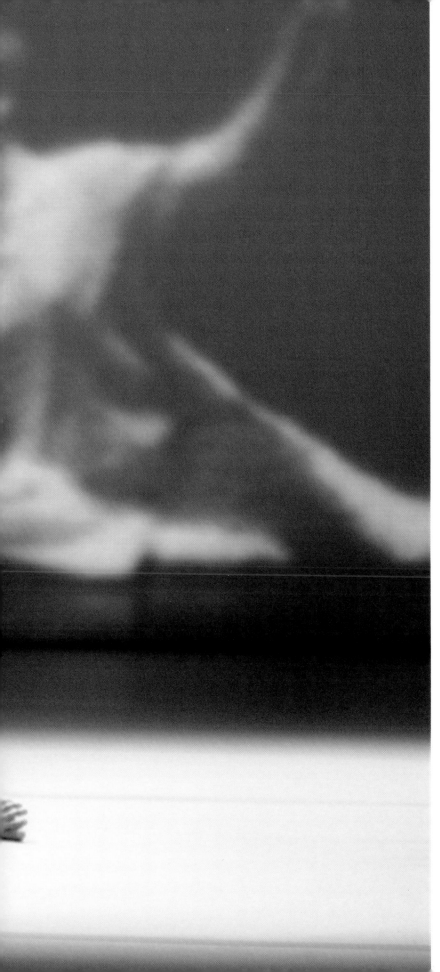

WHITE 2003

WHITE 2003

WHITE 2003

WHITE 2003

WHITE 2003

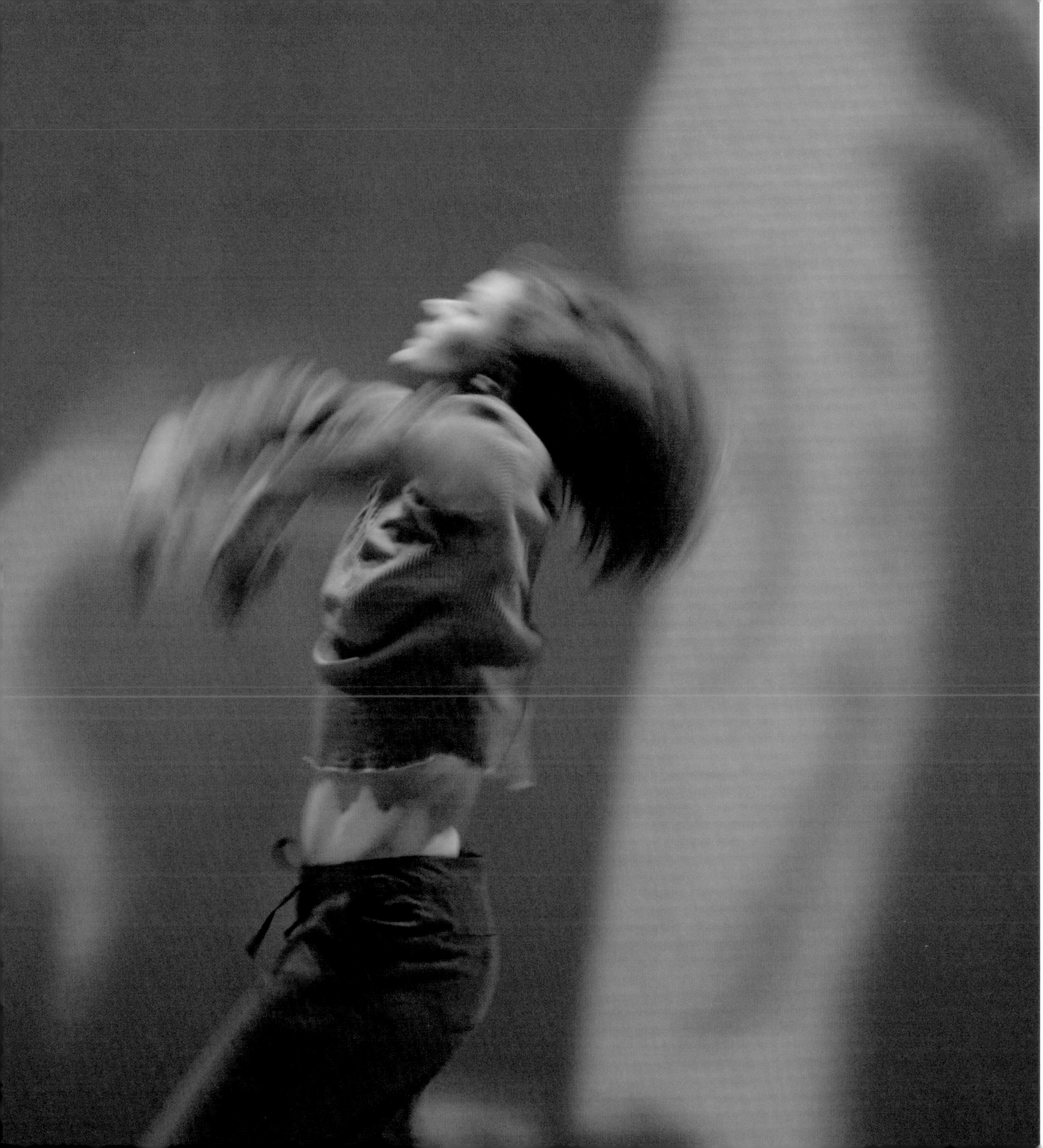

ROSEMARY BUTCHER'S *SCAN* (2000)

SUSAN LEIGH FOSTER

At first you see the grid: four bodies, incessantly in motion, are sliced by bands of light that delineate the space's latitude and longitude.[1] Persisting in their articulateness, body parts emerge from deep shadow into brilliant light, receding instantly into darkness, reappearing dazzlingly illuminated. Almost always, dancers face one of the four sides of the space. Nearly as often, they align themselves one behind another, creating two pairs of dancers who move sagittally across or along the strict stripes of dark and bright. Isolating them from face-to-face interaction while at the same time enmeshing them in a common orientation, the grid-like organisation of the bodies resembles that of urban public space, especially Manhattan. Yet the scale of this space, a mere twenty by twenty feet, makes it feel nothing like a cityscape, but instead an anatomy theatre.

At first what you see is an onslaught of jointedness: vertical, restless, relentless, the bodies pursue a meticulously conceived course of action. Everywhere you look a joint is flexing, sometimes in an effort to indent the body into the surrounding space, sometimes as if to probe the inner mechanics of action itself. Each of the four bodies conducts its own inquiry into the realm of physical potential with matter-of-fact yet fulsome effort. In so doing they engage dance movement as a matter to be manipulated: reiterated, slowed down, reversed, re-oriented… the possibilities are endless.

Less than a minute into the piece, you realise that the generalised articulateness of bodies is contoured by specific lines of inquiry: these bodies are straining to illuminate their insides, pulling the ribcage apart or ploughing the flesh along a vein's path. What is more, they work at opening themselves up in pairs. One body scans or probes another's surfaces. One body assists and supports another, holding, placing, even massaging the other's flesh. In this unorthodox examination, an elbow briefly serves as detecting device; a knee or heel performs an adjustment. Working to determine the essence of bone, vessel, fibre, the dancers generate a plethora of new measurements, lengths and distances but also densities and textures.

Nineteen minutes long, SCAN offers no repetition, no reprise of its action.[2] Pieces of the dancers' individual movement phrases return but always in new relation to adjacent materials. The pace of action registers levels of intensity, from slower to faster or softer to harder and back, but few recognisable breaks in the action occur. The occasional stillness, not a cessation of action, and not a contemplative moment, marks just another tempo in a range of tempos. Unlike the thesis-antithesis-synthesis phrasing of earlier modern dance or the repetitions and resolution of ballet, SCAN maintains a steady urgency. It modulates between energies almost imperceptibly. The size of the actions makes this possible. No moves are huge or minuscule. All moves evidence an exacting span, a precise effort, a complete investment.

Standing behind one another, facing a common direction, the dancers interface between one body's back and the other's front. In this partnering, they assist but also inhibit one another's efforts. Running an arm across shoulder, around head, down the back, one dancer traces the bodily contours of the dancer in front. Filling in the space left vacant by a partner's move, they ghost the efforts of the anterior body. Catching a raised arm and holding it back, they arrest the body's flow. It wriggles away, waits patiently, continues elsewhere – all these tactics for dancing with but also around one another.

Bodies collapse, persist, grasp, hold, yank, push, avoid and submit. Their jointedness renders them capable of interfacing along most surfaces. The degree of complexity and intricacy in their ongoingness is astonishing. The tactility of their grasps, the centred equilibrium with which they move into the new, celebrates the body as fleshly matter. Holding one another from behind, transporting the body to its new location, they grip and manoeuvre the body, not as object, not as subject. Their style, not matter-of-fact, is also not about anything but the physical.

Dancers assist one another, supporting from behind as one falls backwards or sideways, pulling up from the floor to standing, jiggling shoulders as if to relieve tension, stroking the side of the head. But they also disrupt the path of another's motion; they block a gesture's momentum, entangle their own limb with the other body's activity. In these moments, caring assistance slides over into dominance: concern becomes control.

Dancers bear down on one another, almost racing to arrive a hair's breadth prior to their designated encounter. Yet they remain perfectly matched, interrupting or furthering one another's efforts with flawless coordination. Still, their interfaced interlockings evince the sweat and glow of flesh, not the streamlined seamlessness of machinery. Proliferating complexity and intricacy, the dancers explore the idiosyncrasies of corporeality.

Duos change both their facings and positions frequently. Although the two men stand behind more often than the two women, there is no significant difference in their vocabularies, or in the kinds of partnering they undertake. Each bears the gravity of the other's body; carries or pushes or withstands the other's weight.

The music, composed by Cathy Lane, resembles the compressor-like machinations of an iron lung or the cavernous ricochets of sounds that occur inside the MRI chamber. Like the grid, it surrounds and envelops the dancers, inflecting their motion with a more ominous urgency.

From the programme notes you have learned that *SCAN* is inspired, in part, by cultural theorist Lisa Cartwright's book *Screening the Body*. Cartwright surveys the history of medical technologies that have provided ever more detailed images of bodily interiors – what lies beneath the skin, inside the organ and nerve tissue, muscle and bone. Illuminating the insides, these screening devices assist in the 'advancement' of medical diagnosis and treatment, and perhaps more importantly, they manufacture our knowledge of physiological processes, providing newly detailed images of our insides which are then displayed frequently in all varieties of public space.

Absorbed and then distilled within this confined theatrical space, these images become the stuff that preoccupies *SCAN*'s four bodies. Scanning, measuring, probing motions

haunt the choreography. Extruded from and then vanishing inside the ongoingness of movement, these screenings inhabit the same space as the cultural imaginary. They give presence to our fears and fantasies of bodily failings.

Employed with increasing frequency since the 1970s, the grid re-organises individual and social identities along the lines suggested by Michel Foucault's theorisations of personhood and power. Creating nodal points of bodily interaction rather than organic or hierarchised ensembles, the grid displays the grip of power, the faceless totality of its hold on bodies. Conforming to the grid, dancers move along corridors, facing in one of the four cardinal directions. They are enmeshed within a system; they do not define the space, but rather are defined by it. Earlier generations of modern dance choreographers imagined space quite differently. Convinced that individuals working together co-created space, choreographers such as Graham, Humphrey and Weidman cast bodies into arrangements that fused their distinctiveness organically: three standing, two to one side, one on the floor, four others moving away on the diagonal, all connected through dynamic lines of tension. Look at any Barbara Morgan photograph of Graham's early pieces, and you will see the dancers' sculptural coherence as discrete bodies bound in a tensile ensemble. Cunningham blasted this sticky organicism to smithereens with his multi-focused array of bodies randomly strewn throughout the space. Each body, as an equally central focus, commanded the viewer's undivided attention. No longer drawn into the tensile vortices of energy that organic spacing created, the viewer instead drew back in order to apprehend the dancer's equi-valent positions in space. From this detached position, viewers also watch themselves watching, choosing where next to look, treating all movements as equally captivating. The grid retains the non-organic array of Cunningham's choreography, but not the random interactivity among dancers. The grid systematises dancers while retaining their individuatedness.

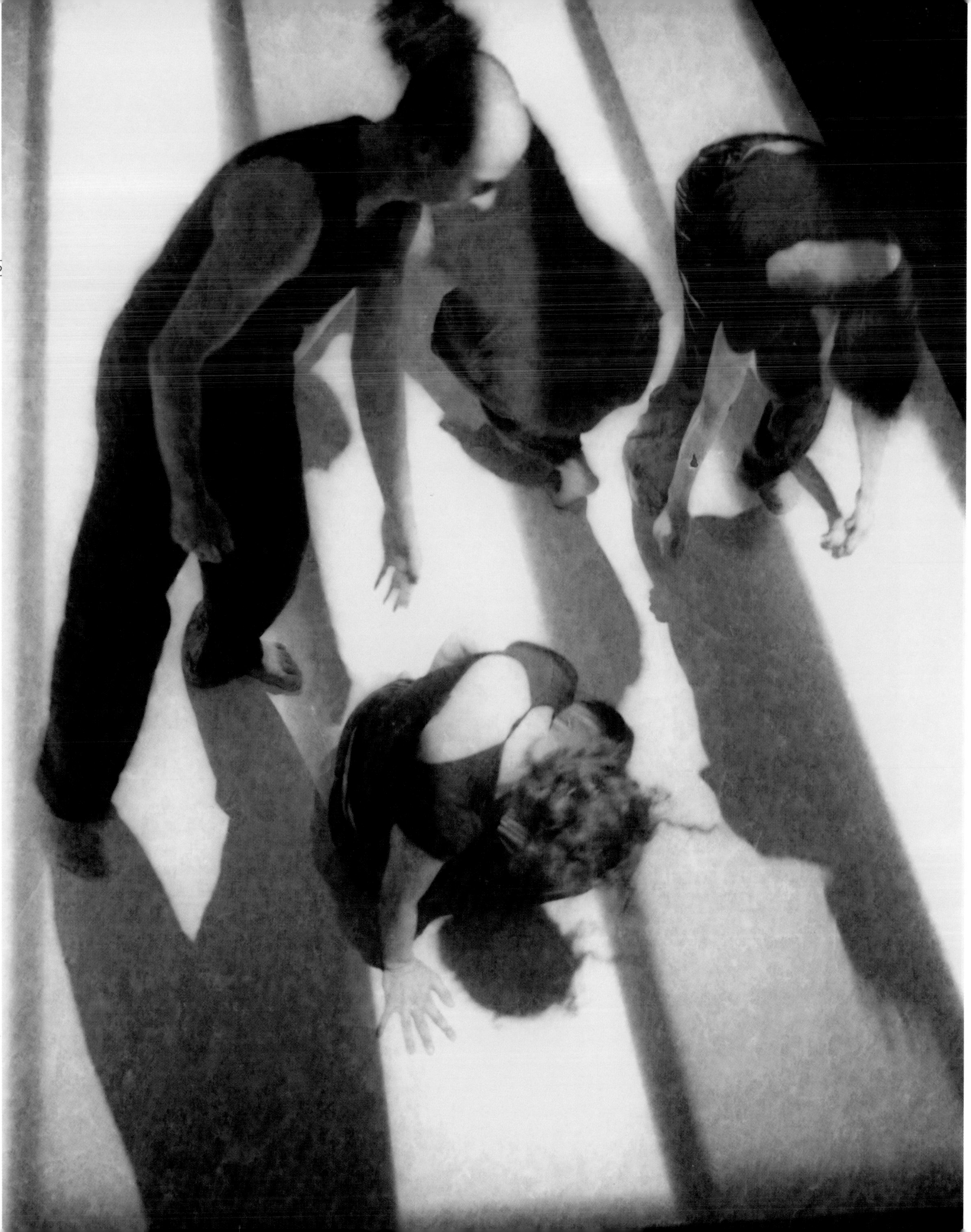

Butcher left London for the grid of Manhattan in 1969. Studying with both Graham and Cunningham, she incorporated the debate between organic and random organisations of bodies. Graham's technique taught the dancer to construct the body as sequentially constructed totality, its parts organised according to a tensile and viscous logic. Cunningham's technique presented the body's potential for articulateness, its parts equally capable of speaking their own mind. Graham's radiating and spiralling floor exercises in the morning; Cunningham's geometric whimsy in the afternoon.[3]

Back in England, Graham's technique was just beginning to be deployed as an antidote to ballet. Its preference for bare-footed connection to the floor, for an exploration of surface-depth relations, opened radical new horizons of choreographic and training possibilities. What other technique came close to constituting itself so defiantly in opposition to the Pythagorean values of ballet? And what other technique offered an entire class-worth of exercises, all developing organically from the basic precepts of the form, none of them replicating any aspect of balletic line or lightness? Limon technique, which Butcher also studied at the University of Maryland on her first trip to the United States, offered the lush resiliency of falling and rebounding, but it modulated, rather than opposed, the pliés, tendus and battements of ballet. Only Graham's technique matched the ballet's potential for re-ordering and varying basic positions and steps while utilising an entirely alternative vocabulary and style.

But in the US, not only had Cunningham unseated the pre-eminence of Graham's modernism, but 1960s experimentation across dance, theatre and the visual arts had begun to interrogate and contest Cunningham's aesthetics. Taking his commitment to the value of physical articulateness to its furthest limits, Judson artists breached the boundaries of vocabulary by proposing that any and all movement could function as the matter from which dance is created. Performance art collectives such as Fluxus applied the visual arts concerns with paint as matter to embodied situations. Theatre collectives such as the Living Theatre and the Open Theatre operated at the interstices between art and life.

Establishing the distinctiveness of their choreographic vision in the early 1960s, many of these artists explored the epistemological consequences of the daily movement – dance movement continuum well into the 1970s. Butcher remembers most especially Trisha Brown's breakthrough piece, *Walking on the Wall* (1971), in which dancers in harnesses walked quite competently across the Whitney Museum walls. Brown cantilevered the body into uncanny, non-normalcy in order to comment on art through daily movement and to enliven life through art. How could walking down the street, much less walking on the stage, ever look the same?

Returning to England in 1969, Butcher was hired by Dartington College to teach Graham technique, but she was hesitant to perpetuate its popularity. Even as it diffused the power and pervasiveness of ballet, it also reinforced many of ballet's elitist values. As Butcher saw it, both Graham technique and ballet championed the exclusivity of dance movement and the hallowed calling of dance training.[4] Returning to New York in 1970 and studying there until 1974, Butcher worked especially closely with Judson choreographer Elaine Summers. Trained in ballet as well as Graham, Limon and Cunningham, Summers had begun to question the process of training through which one's own body becomes imprinted with others' aesthetic visions. Realising that she was living 'according to an energy pattern, a body imagery' that was not hers, she recounts her quest to discover an originary way of moving in these terms:

> I spent a lot of time by myself doing that work, and one summer I felt, 'If I'm really honest about it, all I want to do is lie on the floor. I really don't want to move.' So for two-and-a-half months, during the three-hour period I spent dancing every day, I didn't get up off the floor. And in that time, I began to discover my own energy.[5]

Summers describes a process of voiding out all previous training, simply by lying on the floor and waiting for her own body to initiate a course of action. The new awareness of her own energy that eventually emerged, Summers claims, altered her entire perception of movement and her relation to her surroundings.

Summers' quest to investigate her own energy patterns was guided by a feminist impulse to reclaim a body dominated by more masculinist training procedure and aesthetics.[6] Butcher worked with Summers on an alternative training programme that developed out of her efforts to de-pattern her own body. Calling it kinetic awareness, Summers focused attention on body's weight and economy of emotion rather than its shape. From practising this awareness, Butcher remembers, her body changed, slowly shedding its habits acquired from the study of both Graham and ballet.[7] She also learned film editing from Summers, and was encouraged by her to consider using a film sensibility to guide choreographic decision-making.

Back at Dartington in 1974, Butcher began working alongside Steve Paxton and studied contact improvisation with him. Her conception of dance technique expanded even further. Contact improvisation's democratic invitation to any and all bodies to participate in a mutual discovery of their weight and momentum defied the myth of artist as essentially unique, whether through talent or sensitivity. It also called into question any singular conception of technical competence in dance. As the form makes patently clear, different dance forms require distinctive kinds of training.

Butcher's *SCAN* depicts the 1970s body she acquired from Brown, Summers, Paxton and others, but grown up, wise, aware of the power relations that determine individual and group identities. It celebrates the articulate body and the potential for movement to signify physicality itself rather than any interiorised feelings or desires. Yet, in its commitment to physicality, *SCAN* also summons up the fragility and precariousness of the body, especially as it stands positioned among medical, penal and consumerist disciplinary functions of the state. Perhaps most importantly, it vivifies a commitment to movement as research and to dance-making as a process.

In contrast to the *Spectacular Bodies* exhibition at the Hayward Gallery (running during the same season in which *SCAN* premiered), *SCAN* offers extraordinary ordinary bodies. *Spectacular Bodies* investigates the body as 'an astounding feat of engineering', a complex machine whose parts and workings can be scientifically mapped out in all their detail, whereas Butcher's *SCAN* champions the body's uncapturability. *Spectacular Bodies* presents four centuries of efforts to uncover and pinpoint the body's various functions in time and space, studying its still shapes, calculating its structural and chemical components.**

SCAN stands up to the full force of this investigation with dextrous eloquence. It defies the immense efforts, documented in exhibitions such as *Spectacular Bodies* or *Plastination*, to pin the body down.

In developing *SCAN*, Butcher asked dancers to generate their phrases based on images from Cartwright's book. In addition, she gave them assignments such as 'moving the bones from one location to another, presenting or connecting them' or 'holding onto the skeleton'. These kinds of instructions provoke new coordinations among parts of the body. They cultivate concentration on anatomical organisation as a site for imaginative play.

In the first anatomy theatres, onlookers, who simply paid a fee for admission, surrounded the cadaver on all sides, gazing down on a team of doctors and assistants as they performed the dissection. All eyes were focused on a central inert body which was incapable of contesting, except through the sheer truculence of flesh, the probing inquiries of the living. In *SCAN*, four bodies, very much alive, very much aware of the scrutinising gazes that hold them in their regard, protest the theatre's distribution of power. Non-compliant, they never succumb to exhaustion much less an identifiable ordering of their motions.

Although situated within the grid, *SCAN*'s dancers do not move identically; far from it. Their individual vocabularies seldom repeat, and hardly ever overlap. Organising this diversity, duos, one or both, frequently face a single spatial orientation simultaneously. Then one dancer breaks away, but only to face in the criss-crossing direction. Still, their individuated statements

suggest togetherness, rather than regimentation. These are not clones or drones operating as functionaries in some Western nightmarish projection of communism. They are politically astute agents, dancing out the situation of their embodiedness.

Political theorists Ernesto Laclau and Chantal Mouffe claim that we know ourselves as individuals only through and because of our apprehension of the social.[8] If one were to choreograph their theories of the social, you might see an improvising mass of bodies whose occasional collective achievements – lines, clusters, circles, etc. – enable individuals to actualise themselves, to apprehend their individuatedness. Collectively, dancers might determine what choreographic rules to put in place, what aesthetic presuppositions to follow.

The grid does not provide this kind of potential to make up collectively who we are. More sinister (or realistic?), it specifies each individual's place in relation to the vectors of power that define the whole. Yet it invites the possibility of working together. Not facing each other in a circle or in pairs, not buying into that romantic proposition that we could change the world by looking one another in the eye, SCAN places dancers next to one another, working alongside one another. Even as it summons up some larger organisational pattern of which all the performers are a part, it also suggests the possibility that the dancers, colluding with this pattern, can adapt it to suit their own creative desires. Complic it with the grid's specifications for spatial orientation, the dancers nonetheless conspire together to negotiate difference.

As much as they make evident the grid, SCAN's dancers show us the body's non-conformity to it. They present corporeal effervescence in the face of the massive reductive and invasive technologies that confront the contemporary body. They use the grid to intensify their urgency, to make more apparent their articulateness, to highlight the body's complex ordinariness.

Can we also find in SCAN a metaphor for new notions of the interface between human and machine? The dancers in their pairings, interrupting, assisting, ghosting one another, show us a new model for interactivity. How will the cyborg parts of ourselves interface in the future? SCAN certainly displays all our anxieties, but also the potential playfulness in these oncoming relations with smart houses and cars, with all forms of prostheses.

SCAN proposes to resist the break-up of the body precipitated by invasive medical technologies and increasingly microscopic voyeurism of interiority through the vitality and resilience of urgent motion. It denounces the death of the body promoted by cybertechnologies' seduction through the sweating yet exuberant dedication of dancers' articulateness. Four bodies, urgently in motion, within the anatomy theatre; towards the end two of the dancers walk out of the space, leaving the other two to finish the dance. What you see at the end is that it does not, cannot end.

Scanning SCAN repeatedly, I have endeavoured to sense its architectural and spatial sitedness, its materiality as movement, its disposition and coordination of physicalities, and its sequencing of events. These four choreographic elements are bound together in Butcher's work as intimately, complexly and elegantly as SCAN's four dancers. Entwined in this (metaphoric) 'text',[9] these four perspectives on dance construct a textual quartet that calls out, across the irreconcilability of dancing and writing, to her dance.

Endnotes

1. My reading of SCAN is based on a studio performance of the piece I witnessed in November 2000 and the video created by Vong Phaophanit with Greg Pope, which shows the lighting and staging of the piece.

2. The full piece is thirty-one minutes in length, including nineteen minutes of dance and a twelve-minute film. I was not able to view the film, projected onto the floor where the dancers perform, which followed the danced portion of the piece. For an account of that film and its relation to the dance, see Gladstone, N. 'Rosemary Butcher's SCAN', Dance Theatre Journal, 2000, 16, 2: pp.8-11.

3. Butcher recalls fondly Cunningham's classes in his studio without heating on 3rd Avenue. Students routinely wore hats and gloves during class. Interview with Rosemary Butcher by the author, 24 November 2000.

4. Interview with Rosemary Butcher, 24 November 2000.

5. Elaine Summers quoted in Ellen Webb, 'Teaching from the inside out', Soho Weekly News, 2 August 1979, 51.

6. Butcher recalls that Summers introduced her to Kate Millett and other feminists and intellectuals. Interview with Rosemary Butcher, 24 November 2000.

7. Interview with Rosemary Butcher, 24 November 2000.

8. For an excellent introduction to Laclau's and Mouffe's claims see Community at Loose Ends, Miami Theory Collective (eds.), Minneapolis: University of Minnesota, 1991.

9. Editor's note: the notion that dance, viewed by an expert spectator, might be identified by that spectator, at the turn of the 21st century, as 'text', signals the tenacity of what has been called the 'textual turn', which re-models even embodied art practices, from the spectator's position, in textual terms - seeking then to seem to be able to 'read' them.

FIVE SIDED FIGURE 1979

IMPRINTS 1983

UNBROKEN VIEW 1995

BORDER COUNTRY:
LOOKING AT ROSEMARY
BUTCHER'S WORK

UNBROKEN VIEW 1995

FROM A VISUAL ARTS PERSPECTIVE

HUGH STODDART

Rosemary Butcher doesn't go to see dance very much, but she visits a lot of galleries. Her formative experience, as other writers in this collection also indicate, was working at Judson Church in the late 1960s and spending time in New York in the early 1970s; her encounters with people like Robert Rauschenberg and Philip Glass, Trisha Brown and Yvonne Rainer she freely acknowledges as highly significant. She has had, it seems to me, a life-long feeling of identification with fine art practice whilst remaining an impassioned devotee of the infinite possibilities of the human body as a source of expression. This had made for a struggle: firstly, because her own personal demon is that she wants 'to make things' but hasn't, at least until now, *quite* had the feeling of having done so and, secondly, because her particular approach to choreography has often been placed on the margins of 'dance' as a defined area in terms of funding and support.

A fine art sensibility, then: Butcher pushes at the studio door. She tries to get as close as she can to that feeling of 'making things'. She thinks of her choreographic work, though rooted in improvisation in terms of actual process with the dancers, as being more akin to a painter who scrapes away paint then replaces it with more. The painting is thus achieved by accretion, the traces of previous working at the surface remaining as an accumulation of striving, a weighty evidence… I was writing recently about the abstract painter George Blacklock, and though I apologise for quoting from myself, I do so because this kind of language seems so appropriate when talking about Butcher's art:

> The canvas can be thought of as a kind of photographic paper retaining evidence of the artist's endeavour. The scale of the paintings is appropriate to his own body. The swirling shapes which occur again and again seem likewise to be a record of their making: they are pregnant with movement. Blacklock makes them seem so satisfyingly considered and the product of great care and control yet they possess the obsessive physicality of a doodle, that mysterious vigour of something that has leapt, pristine, from the uniqueness of a single sensibility.[1]

Butcher often refers to 'space' – again, this is a visual artist-like attitude, reminding me of remarks made by Ron Haselden, an artist with whom Butcher has worked on two occasions.[2] Whether he's making work for a gallery or for another place (he has a very established practice as an artist working on public sites) the nature of 'the space' is always the starting point.[3] In the case of *Body as Site* (1992-3), for example, the dancers were in a sense *working with* the artists Butcher had brought into the piece; as a totality, dancers, sculptures and choreography together absolutely occupied the space, reaching out and animating every last bit of it – and shared that space with us, the audience. The dancers brought bodies, the artists had left sites. In the first part, when I saw it performed, dancer Henry Montes took up beautiful positions, seeming to cling, upside down, to the walls like a lizard while another, Fin Walker, had her own motif of a scuttling movement along the floor like a creature on the sea bed. To set such anthropomorphic moves against a precise mathematical form and the neatness of the gallery space created a wonderful dialogue, an illuminating collision.

One of the dilemmas with which Rosemary grapples is that on the one hand she wants to reach out to the space, to engage with that architectural framing of choreography, and on the other hand she needs a clarity, a lack of clutter of irrelevant detail. A temporary occupation of space which is likely to be full of such detail (the 'empty warehouse' syndrome, in other words, the kind of space Robert Wilson might be happy to take on) is not for her. Again, her sensitivity to space means that she prefers not to present work in a theatrical environment where space has been zoned; that is to say, where part of it is declared to be for spectacle (the stage) and other parts declared to be invisible (backstage, offstage, blacked out ceilings, etc.), while a third part is for the audience (front of house). All this means, in sum, is that what she *really* wants is a gallery, the proverbial white space – and that is hard to find. It shouldn't be, but it is: crossover is more talked about than actively embraced. The problems which often arise can be quite technical, problems of practicality: galleries are typically not structured to accommodate real-time based work which needs rehearsal, preparation, fees, ticket sales, etc.… and then Health and Safety starts to loom and fire exits have to be considered… and then the whole nature of what Butcher wants, which is an intimate contract between watcher and dancer based on a simple democracy of shared space, becomes fraught with difficulty.

UNBROKEN VIEW 1995

FRACTURED LANDSCAPE
FRAGMENTED NARRATIVES
1995
Film: Noel Bramley

Collaboration and related issues

The tradition in fine art is to focus on the individual. Famously Christo 'came out' as a partnership when he and his partner Jeanne-Claude declared, many years after international fame had been achieved, that 'Christo' was both of them, a kind of corporate identity. Since then other 'partnerships' have emerged and some have been very notable, be they twins, siblings, lovers or friends. But in a sense such partnerships remain *an individual* – separate elements in the finished work are not separately claimed.

Butcher has been noted for her collaborations – not, it has to be said, with other choreographers, but rather with people established in other areas – be it music, architecture or art – particularly, and most notably, art. I want to focus on this in the context of Rosemary Butcher's work because it brings us by another route to the fact that she has chosen to occupy a difficult terrain we could sketchily entitle 'between dance and art'. I have to admit, too, that collaboration has been a major element in my own practice as a writer working in cinema and television and gives me, I think, an insight into both the positive and negative aspects of it. I think as well that film/video is of particular significance in looking at Butcher's work now, a point I'd like to return to later.

Whatever her doubts – to which I also return later in this chapter – Butcher has, it seems to me, embraced at least to some degree both the stimulus and the restriction of what I would call collaboration, and I hope she will forgive my persistence on the point… Artists like Anya Gallacio and Ron Haselden, with both of whom Butcher has worked, had well developed practices and certain ways of working, certain preoccupations which accorded with things Butcher herself was wanting to work with and hence her approach to them. With specific regard to *Body as Site*, she asked them to provide 'sites' in which her dancers could work and, in the case of Gallacio's sculpture particularly, this set up considerable restrictions on the moves which the dancers could make given the clinging nature of the horsehair which covered the floor. Rosemary accepted those restrictions, she worked with them.

Body as Site involved the contributions of four artists and one of them, Paul Eliman, led to what seemed to me a simple but inspired idea which was to place a grid of road markers ('cats' eyes') on the floor of the gallery in which three dancers then performed. Like the game of 'battleships' I played as a child, it was a grid of dots and thus the dancers could make lines, and endlessly shifting ones at that. Perhaps this idea emerged from the kind of mutual searching often characteristic of collaboration?

Collaboration is not easy. It is not friendship, necessarily, though it might encompass it. Rather it is a matter of creative conflict. That is not to imply shouting necessarily, though it might include that. It is rarely, if I may say so, a matter of equality. Personalities have different weights. Indeed one only has to look at the dancers in many of Butcher's works to see those weights in disposition before one's eyes: the duality of the conflict/collaboration often lies very deep in the work. This is powerfully in evidence in *Fractured Landscapes, Fragmented Narratives* (1997, 2002), which explores, via Butcher's intense engagement with physicality, issues of dependence and trust, revealed vividly by the interactions between two dancers. The image referred to earlier of an upside down figure is found here too, but in an enormously different way: instead of the solitary engagement of one figure with a wall, we have a charged entanglement, with one dancer literally holding/held by the other – feet to shoulders, hands to ankles. I have spoken (nervously) of that particular piece as 'dealing pre-eminently with *angoisse*'.[4] But Rosemary herself was ready to accept that comment. She has said of her work that 'the physicality is the driving force' but she is nonetheless happy to acknowledge the emotion lying within it, and indeed speaks of 'the need for it to be exposed'.

Talking to Rosemary recently, I found that she now doubts 'whether she has ever truly collaborated' – by which she means, I think, that she has never quite been in the position of working with someone on a basis of completely shared endeavour, and more crucially, not in a position of complete equality. But are such collaborations perhaps only made in heaven?

How does any creative work come about? One might pose this as a rather foolishly over-generalised question. Heaven was characterised by Talking Heads as 'a place where nothing ever happens' but let's float into that celestial studio – and there we find the individual creates something and there it is: the painting, the sculpture, the whatever. Art history is a process of reinforcing this paradigm: collaborations go in final chapters, add-ons… But in the real world with all its mess and muddle and love and hate and pressures and glories, what might one's answer to that foolish question be? We interact, we exchange, we borrow.

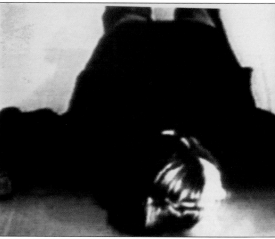

FRACTURED LANDSCAPE
FRAGMENTED NARRATIVES
1995
Film: Noel Bramley

FRACTURED LANDSCAPE
FRAGMENTED NARRATIVES
1995

AFTER THE CRYING AND THE SHOUTING 1989

I see collaboration as a mutual sifting – one person places stuff on the table and another person is sifting through, accepting some things, rejecting others. They are like dealers. This is arguably true too of the working relationship Butcher has with her dancers – particularly so with a piece like *Fractured Landscapes*. It is such a personal piece, about such intimate communication between the dancers that in re-presenting the piece with different dancers, the piece has to be rebuilt anew, though the essentials remain.

Butcher's inspiration is such, I suspect, that she needs the dancers she works with to help to articulate the ideas which she brings as inchoate beginnings, to help those ideas 'become form' – to borrow from the title of a famous exhibition.[5] As another artist said to me once, 'We don't know what we're looking for until we find it.' This would mean, if I'm right, that Butcher needs her dancers to be very generous, she needs them to be creative yet ready to surrender that creativity. This is akin to what is required of the actors who work with Mike Leigh.

But collaboration is, as Butcher has said to me, very time-consuming. Moreover, it can leave one pent up with the feeling that without it, one might have done better, mistakes might have been avoided. We return to that dealing table if only in our anxious memories, we sift through the stuff again and perhaps we forget the good we took from the other side of that table and our minds instead close tightly over things we let go at the instigation, or so we remember it, of the other partner.

Our culture is increasingly posited on the individual. In the arts, therefore - where marketing is as crucial as it is with everything else - to attach any created thing firmly to an individual is increasingly the preferred option. There has emerged in recent years, in the world of cinema, something known as 'the possessory credit'. That is to say that we find a person's name above the film title with an apostrophe 's' after it, or a phrase like 'A Roman Polanski film'. In the twenty-first century, the biggest issue with which we shall tussle will be intellectual property rights. Billions are spent already on securing patents, on trying to sew up ideas so that they can be controlled and sold as clean goods with no claims being made by others. Our culture is also increasingly occupied with 'being creative'. Everybody wants to be creative: the booming subjects at universities are those which encompass such longings. When these two tendencies come together, we are likely to find tensions. Who is to be credited? Who claims what? At the serious end of the spectrum, there can be heartache, not least because we live in very competitive times, and one's 'credits' become crucial.

Perhaps sensing these things, Butcher wants more and more to be completely in control of her work and she characterises the future she wishes to map out as one in which she might be working more with technicians rather than with people possessing what one might term a definable artistic identity. In other words, she sees collaboration – no matter to what degree she has engaged in it – as something she is leaving behind. She wants, one might say, to push herself closer to that paradigm which has arguably haunted her – the artist in the studio.

Flying solo! These issues might resolve themselves in a shift by this choreographer towards the wonders of computers, so that the 'physicality' she speaks of, that essential inspiration, becomes raw material, captured digitally and then available to be worked on and shaped subsequently. Having myself worked in the theatre, I know that I return to film as my first love because it is something that is *built* rather than something that *happens* (even if, as the screenwriter, I'm not that much on site once the footings have gone into the ground). The screened material in *Fractured Landscapes* may be a clue to where Rosemary is headed. The ice white squares of light projected down on to the floor in *Still-Slow-Divided* (2002) could be taken as additional signposts – they are as close to cinema screens as one can get, and the dancers enter and leave the frame as if it were film.

This observation puts me powerfully in mind of *After the Last Sky* (1995), a piece Butcher first showed at the Royal College of Art. Because I thought this such a fine piece, and one which embodied both the dilemmas and the triumphs of Butcher's practice, I have reproduced below my review of it, with the kind permission of *Frieze* magazine. And though it was several years ago, I still think it might be a pointer to the future…

It is not for me to speculate where Rosemary Butcher is headed. Wherever it is, though, that she *does* turn out to be headed, she will doubtless take a trail which takes her across difficult terrain, just as she has always done. Doubtless, too, others will not allow the jungle to grow over the path she has taken: they'll be following.

In this publication, we are also looking back, in celebration of a career of many years duration, and in that spirit I'd like to conclude by giving the final word to George Blacklock, about whom I wrote above – himself of much the same generation as Rosemary and, indeed, of myself. Much has been accumulated…

> An artist's work isn't necessarily about what he or she says it's about. Artists *hope* their work is about what they want it to be about but there's always an undertow. We are unreliable witnesses… But we mean everything, we meant it all, and that can be frightening when we look back on it.

Endnotes

1   Meridiano de Greenwich, Madrid and touring UK 2002

2   *After the Crying and the Shouting* (1989), *Body as Site* (1992-3)

3   *Art and Architecture*, no.53, 1999

4   Taped interview, March 2002

5   *When attitude becomes form*, Berne and London, 1969-70

AFTER THE CRYING AND THE SHOUTING 1989

AFTER THE LAST SKY

Review from *Frieze* Magazine, no.21, 1995

This piece, running continuously over a week, consisted of four large screens forming an enclosing square, on which were video-projected sequences of six dancers: choreographed by Rosemary Butcher, filmed and edited by David Jackson, and accompanied by a soundtrack composed by Simon Fisher-Turner. The piece ran for twenty minutes but you need to see it through more than once. Sometimes you were watching the same shot of the same dancer simultaneously on more than one screen, sometimes shots from different angles of the same dancer, sometimes different dancers whose moves echoed one another: a complex rhythm was thus set up creating an interaction across the four screens. In addition to the dancers, there were stills of spectacular skies (sunsets) – they marked the opening of each of the four sections of the piece and also were sometimes laid in slow moving and colliding blocks over the monochromes images of the dancers, beneath which the dancers remained visible. For filming the dancers, the camera was always fixed, both in position and focus, for each shot. In evolving the choreography, Butcher specified that many movements executed by the dancers should last a fixed time: each 'enters' the camera's frame, carries out the movement, then leaves. No movement is ended by an editing cut. The movements were simple, precise, repeated. What you heard was sometimes voices, street sounds, bells (recorded in Israel) but mostly it was music - this was composed, as with a film soundtrack, to fit with the completed video sequences.

Video projectors are improving, but the finest remain prohibitively expensive. Those available for After the Last Sky gave us the usual rather 'soft' images – a little inadequate both in respect of the skies and the dance sequences. I took a sneak look at the monitors and saw images of glowing intensity – dancers magically appearing and leaving a black box like something from the earliest history of cinema. It may have been because the screen images were dimmer and less defined than this, it was decided to lower the ambient light: this lent a theatricality to the piece I felt rather inappropriate. The intention was that the audience should move around in the space – thus experiencing both images and sounds altering. The screens were built some three feet from the floor to encourage this. I noticed, though, most people just sat on the floor, generally in one of the corners, and remained in one spot throughout. They appeared to feel they were watching a filmed performance rather than entering a created space, an environment, in which it's legitimate to come and go and not worry about standing in front of another 'member of the audience' nor worry about what you're doing with your shadow. Contemporary dance has, of course, 'interfaced' with art for many years – but often all a choreographer really wants from an artist is a backdrop to their dancers. Butcher has worked with several artists and created work mainly for galleries or other non-theatrical spaces. She is very open to what an artist wants to do (or, in this case, a film-maker and a composer) – she puts her own choreographer's sensibility under a kind of fruitful pressure. Butcher's interest currently seems to be the recorded image – the directed image, and in the reduction and concentration which is then possible in choreography. More is less. Her interest is in the multiplicity of image too and its scale and form of presentation. She is asserting the primacy of recorded material. It yields more that what is on the videotape or the soundtape: witnessing these sounds and images is no less an experience than going to a theatre to watch a dance performance.

The title After the Last Sky comes from a text by Edward Said about Palestine (and the accompanying photographs by John Mohr) but this was only a starting point: Said's themes of oppression, containment and, particularly, exile were only perceptible if you gave the choreography a close reading. Butcher eschews drama; her interest is more sculptural: it lies in a reductive attention to the most ordinary movements of the human body, and the precision of them, the display of forces in equilibrium which a body can achieve and then repeat. The figures we watch going through their moves on the screens are closed (not seeing us, not seeing each other), private and yet revealing to us – because they are not trying to show us anything we cannot see. They seem to say 'this is all we have, all we are allowed – our bodies and the clothes we stand up in.'

FLYING LINES
Prep work, Hampstead Heath, 1986

FLYING LINES
Prep work, Hampstead Heath, 1986

FLYING LINES 1986

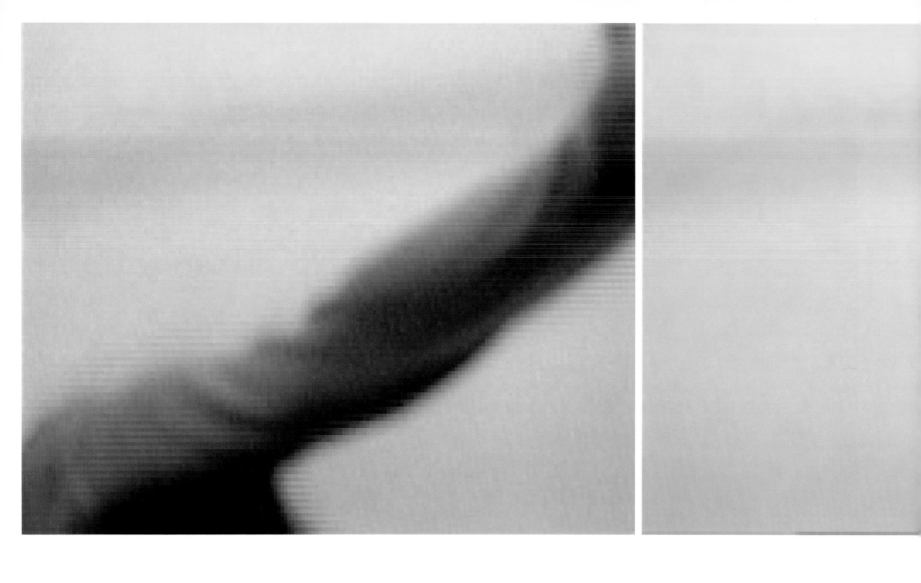

THE RETURN 2004
Dancer: EUN-HI KIM, Film: MARTIN OTTER

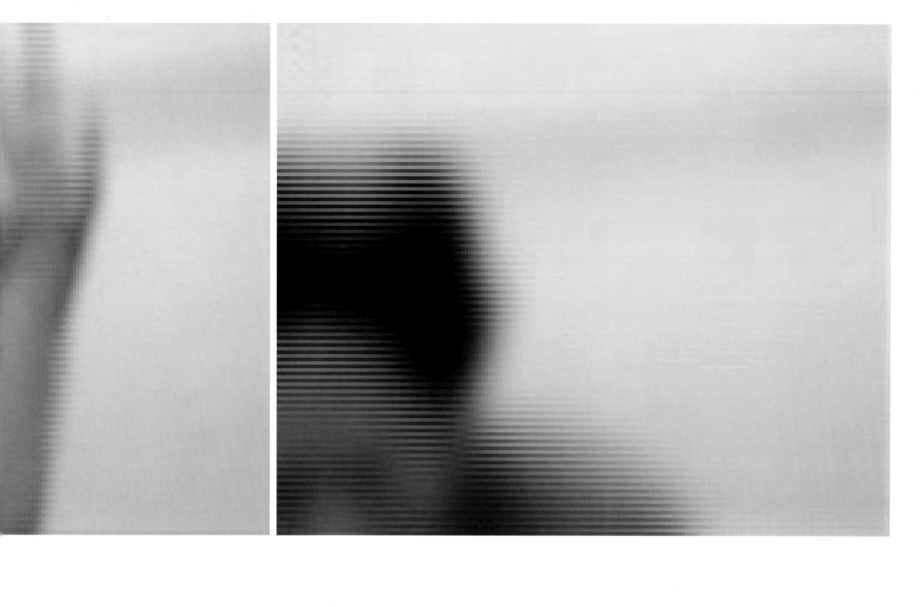

THE RETURN 2004
Dancer: EUN-HI KIM, Film: MARTIN OTTER

THE RETURN 2004
Dancer: EUN-HI KIM, Film: MARTIN OTTER

A 'CONVENTIONAL SUBVERSIVE'?

JOSEPHINE LEASK

When asked why she does what she does, Rosemary Butcher replies that the creative world is a place where she feels sane, where she can sort things out and make 'order out of chaos'. While she still treads on uncertain ground, lives with the fear of failure and the vulnerability that is inherent in making work, she claims today to feel that she has survived.

After three decades of making new work, Butcher admits that it has taken her until now to arrive at a place where she is comfortable. She points out that making work later in life suits her, that her maturity gives her confidence to go ahead and take risks. When asked about the recently greater recognition of her work, Butcher replies that she has benefited from art's rediscovery of the 1970s.

Rosemary Butcher has always presented a complex and ambiguous image to the dance world. Through her incorporation of many of the processes used by the New York new dance artists of the 1960s and 1970s, she has been heralded as the choreographer who brought Judson's aesthetic to a British audience. By way of contrast, she refers to herself as a 'conventional subversive'; a mature choreographer who makes work that constantly challenges traditional dance aesthetics.

Rosemary Butcher's work seems to inhabit the margins of the UK dance world, striving 'to change the way the body is represented' and 'break down processes in [her] search to find new energies in dance'. She has been quietly persistent in her work rather than prominently vocal, which has both earned her respect and made her invisible to certain sections of the dance community. Funding bodies and critics have struggled to understand and define her work, as she has tended to cross into other art forms.

As a professional artist, Butcher is a survivor. She has developed her work with an explicit emphasis on the process of research and development rather than on final product, and she works by asking questions rather than succumbing to dance trends and styles. Ironically, the fact that Butcher claims often to feel like an outsider gives her a certain security, since it means that she is not in competition with others in the dance world. Rosemary Butcher has kept a cool distance from the dance professions, claiming in conversation that she feels more comfortable with the worlds of visual arts and architecture, both of which, she argues, relate directly to real life. Dance, she claims, in its privileging of youth and beauty, its competitive and ephemeral nature, and its inward looking preoccupations, encourages artists to be both immature and self-obsessed - an opinion that was formed through her own experiences as a young dancer. Butcher has said that during her early dance training, she was always more interested in ideas than technique and performance, and was made to feel mediocre because she was not perceived to shine as a performer.

Rosemary Butcher argues that the visual arts are appealing to her because they possess a self-sufficiency that movement does not have. The video arts, for example, can show an image or action which can stand on its own and communicate, whereas if a choreographer wanted to make a piece simply about running, she or he would have to work with other layers of meaning in order to reach a similar level of communication. A video artist, like Bill Viola, 'can present images of someone drowning or burning and demonstrate the thing itself',[1] but this directness is more difficult to achieve through work with the dancer's physical body. In Viola's work *Millennium*, for example, where bodies are seen descending and ascending through water, Butcher argues that he manages to depict the struggle of the human condition through timing, light and strong images, and through the juxtaposition of the human body and water. As important to her work are a number of 20th-century artists who have had the courage to push the boundaries of their own art forms with rigour: Gillian Wearing for her psychological manipulation of filmic images; video artist Gary Hill; theatre director Robert Wilson whose work she considers touches the human spirit; and Peter Brook who pursues his own philosophy of a total theatre from the Bouffes du Nord in Paris. Joseph Beuys has challenged the notion of the art work as 'product', and the film-maker Tarkovsky frames shots in such a way as to allow him to deal with childhood and memory, space and time.

Rosemary Butcher's approach to her work might well seem to be closer to the working methods of visual artists than it is to choreographic tradition. She is interested in real space and time, rather than in the theatrical and the fictional. Using processes of layering and material transformation, she works with the performer's body as an artist might in painting or sculpture. The work rarely appears in theatrical dance venues because proscenium stages and theatrical spaces are both limiting and they impose themselves on the work. Her work has tended instead to be spatially led, where the immediate spatial situation and setup has tended to determine how her dancers move. She has preferred in the past to present performance work as installation or in large architectural structures and outdoor settings. That sort of work has tended to bring an audience of visual artists, architects and composers - a number of whom have become her collaborators.

Butcher was one of the few British choreographers living in New York during the dance boom in the 1970s, and describes the period as one of the most important in her life. She was drawn to site-specific performance, radical questioning of the trained dancer's body, dismissal of narrative and a preoccupation with representation and 'meaning', and to a focus on process rather than product. In this, she was powerfully influenced by the working processes of choreographers like Trisha Brown, Steve Paxton, Yvonne Rainer, Meredith Monk and Lucinda Childs. She cites early Cunningham as a major source of technical information about the body and notes the impact of his structuring devices, which according to Stephanie Jordan were 'non-climactic, non-developmental and open-ended'.[2]

Writing about her time in the US, Butcher noted that the dance world in England, by way of contrast at that time, seemed antagonistic or at best indifferent to the philosophy she sought to embrace.[3] On her return to England, Butcher drew, in her early pieces, on many of the ways of working of these New York artists, inviting

THE RETURN 2004
Dancer: EUN-HI KIM
Film: MARTIN OTTER

dancers to be creative in the work, exploiting a relaxed rather than stylised bodywork and an everyday or pedestrian movement. She explored improvisation to generate material, collaborated with practitioners of other art forms and presented work in non-theatre contexts. Early work with her company, founded in 1975, explored movement that was both athletic and expansive, reacting to particular spaces. It was Judson's conceptual invention that inspired Butcher to 'bring a consciousness of real sensations into choreography', exploring the ordinary and the banal, and how real-life sensations might invade a medium which has otherwise been codified and stylised.

While Butcher was familiar and comfortable with the new dance that was emerging in Dartington and London in the 1970s in the form of the X6 Dance Collective, she had a tentative relationship with the British new dance scene and distanced herself from the political drives which motivated much of the collective's work, such as its obsessive interest in the 'body politic'. Whereas artists such as Emilyn Claid and Jackie Lansley were concerned that dance should 'relate to the social context', Butcher insisted, according to Stephanie Jordan, that she was simply searching for 'pure abstract form'.[4] Butcher admits that, unlike female choreographers who made feminist work in response to the feminist revolution of the time, she did not overtly engage with feminism and kept away from issues which exposed the personal. Just as she steered clear of making work about herself, so she confessed to finding boring much of the contemporary issue-based work that

was driven by 'emotional break-down, sex or drugs'. Instead, she was interested in subtle shifts in movement, space and light, and the body's physical relationship to contexts, environments and other objects. Butcher has recently observed, however, that her identity as a woman has influenced her work in more indirect ways - for example, in her non-linear, multi-layered, fluid working process.

The aesthetic which was developing in the early works employed reduced movement with a focus on geometrical lines often made through skipping patterns and floor patterns of straight lines, right angles, arcs and circles. Butcher has described her early work as 'a kinetic, sculptural experience' that drew the viewer's eye to body designs and group arrangements. In these works, Jordan has noted, the dancers were seen as distributions in space rather than single identities.[5] It was this use of space in her work, as well as the moments of stillness, that allowed the viewer the space to observe; to contemplate the many images which gradually unfolded in the execution of simple steps and pedestrian movement. As Dodds has observed in *Dance Theatre Journal*, Butcher's use of repetition and variation 'carefully constructs layers of movement so that slowly, subtle textures and spatial patterns evolve'.[6] Certain themes began to emerge in her work, such as the theme of incompletion, conveyed by minimal movement and open-endedness. This was evidenced in works which did not have a resolution and in which the dancers came and went, leaving impressions or traces behind them.

As a result of its content, pared-down aesthetics,

anonymity of the performers' identity, use of space and brief lifespan, Butcher's work has a purity and freshness about it. Such qualities have also led to the work being described in terms of an 'uncompromising formalism'[7] that does not pander to dance trends or fashion. Some critics have often dismissed the work as cool or distancing, inaccessible, bland and lacking in emotion, and have found her aesthetics stark and too demanding to watch. However, this very aesthetic, plus the monumental contexts in which the work is shown, have created a spectacle marked by a strong sense of the spiritual.

> The D triptych – 2D (1989-90), a collaboration with architect John Lyall and composer Jim Fulkerson – was performed in Spitalfields Cathedral, East London, where the nave was turned into a performance space with high catwalks down each aisle. Framed by the huge arches like saints, dancers appeared on the catwalks moving their arms very slowly, while other dancers ran down the nave swinging their arms vigorously, alternating between running and walking. There was something spiritually uplifting and mesmerising about the dancers positioned on high, moving with a statuesque solemnity, while those below performed simple mechanical movements at high speed, creating a heaven and earth within the rambling cathedral. It was as if the whole work was gradually rising to the sublime.

Whereas Butcher was 'finding form' in her early stages as a choreographer, in the 1980s she started to produce work that built on the previous years but which moved into greater scale in terms of space and breadth of ideas. These works were generated through collaborations with artists from other media, including architects Zaha Hadid and John Lyall; artists Heinz Dieter Pietsch and Anya Gallacio; and composers Jim Fulkerson and Michael Nyman. Butcher talks about her collaborators as researchers who come up with solutions to the choreographic problems she poses, eventually creating an environment for her movement ideas.

Just as Butcher sees her collaborators as researchers who help her create the right kind of environment, she relies on her dancers as a source of movement material, which she will then direct and shape. She builds up a special relationship with each dancer and spends a considerable amount of time with them in the devising process, getting them to find their own movement solutions through her instructions, so that they develop a stronger commitment to the work. She selects dancers who are often established choreographers and performers, and who are highly technical and mature in outlook. While her work does not require virtuosic technique, it demands considerable understanding of the body and movement, and stamina for the many repetitions, stillnesses and balances. She describes her core group of dancers as being 'intelligent rebels'; those who escaped from a conventional ballet or contemporary training at institutions such as The Royal Ballet. Most of her dancers describe working with Butcher as being a hard, intense, but fascinating journey. Over the years, they have included Julyen Hamilton, Janet Smith, Gaby Agis, Lauren Potter, Dennis Greenwood, Gill Clarke, Russell Maliphant, Jonathan

Burrows, Fin Walker and Henry Montes.

Butcher's work in the 1990s began to employ more narrative content and developed a sense of 'situation', a realisation of where the human body stands in the world, rather than the complete abstraction of previous works. An example of this development was seen in the film installation *After the Last Sky* (1995): this event was based on emotional exile and occupation, and was inspired by the text of the Palestinian post-colonial theorist Edward Said. The thematic and formal shift was reflected in a shift in her working processes: instead of giving them numbers to count or other pedestrian tasks, she would give instructions to her dancers through imagery.

From the early postmodern reflexivity of her work, Rosemary Butcher has shifted through traditional modernism and the worlds of architecture and the visual arts to what has been in recent years a contemporary preoccupation with the human body.

SCAN (2000) uses the body as topic, and images reflect on bone and muscles, suggesting X-ray examination. Butcher was deeply affected by Lisa Cartwright's book, *Screening the Body,* containing descriptions of women's illnesses picked up through early X-rays. It relates the horror of discovering the shadow of disease in the body, and suggests the humiliation of women probed and investigated, then put under the intense scrutiny of the X-ray.

The dancers are suspended in a world of catching, body-dependency and risk-taking movement. The high speed of performance takes the mechanical movement to an emotional peak, suggesting anxiety and panic. The contained performance area is lit (by visual artist Vong Phaopanit) with bands or sections of light, and sodium lights which turn on and off at various stages.

Four dancers perform live with the audience seated at close quarters on four sides. In such close contact, you can see every nerve twitching as the dancers catch, lean onto or manipulate each other. The lifts seem to embody the 'struggle of the human condition' that concerns Butcher. Themes are suggested by metaphors of light, shadow and darkness, as the dancers move into and out of the scrutinising illumination of a sodium light. A soundscore of anxious gasping, composed by Cathy Lane, adds to the intensity and urgency of the piece. Butcher herself is in the film projected into the space at the end of the piece, watching and giving instructions, recalling Tadeusz Kantor's presence in his performance work in the 1980s.

The work has become more intensely expressionistic and also sensual, with a focus on the architecture of the (performing) body, rather than that of space or material structure. Butcher claims that by choosing to explore the intrinsic workings of the (dancer's) body, like a camera zooming in, she has returned to 'form', and is now coming closer to the nature of making dance work.

Endnotes

1   R. Butcher, 'What's past is prologue', *Dance Theatre Journal*, 14(X), 17-21, 1999, p.20

2   S. Jordan, 'Rosemary Butcher', *Striding Out*, London: Dance Books, 1992, pp.160-181

3   R. Butcher 1999, 'What's past is prologue', *Dance Theatre Journal*, 14(X), 17-21, 1999, p.20

4   S. Jordan, 'Rosemary Butcher', *Striding Out*, London: Dance Books, 1992, pp.160-181

5   Ibid, p.172

6   S. Dodds, 'The momentum continues', *Dance Theatre Journal*, Volume 13 (X), 1997, pp. 6-9

7   Ibid, p.9

VANISHING POINT 2004

VANISHING POINT 2004

THE SITE
Prep work, Butler's Wharf, 1983

THE SITE 1983

THE SITE 1983

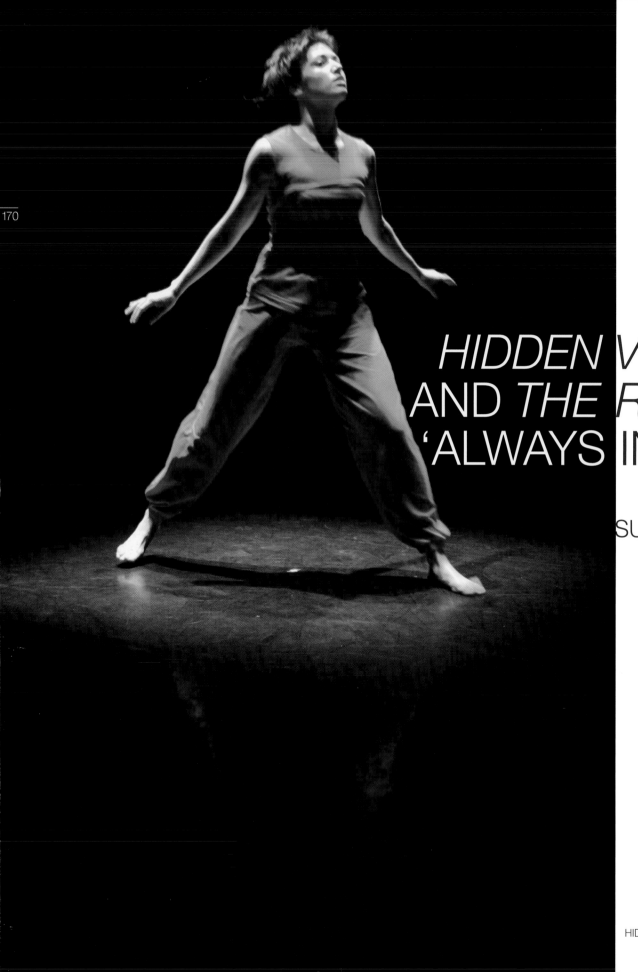

HIDDEN VOICES (2004) AND *THE RETURN* (2005) 'ALWAYS INNOVATE...'

SUSAN MELROSE

managed over the years, despite its acknowledged 'difficulty', its reticences, its occasional severity, to seem to touch some at least of its spectators, working *affectively,* when its maker has argued, over a similar period of time, that she works with the material, rather than with the abstract, the concrete, rather than the affective?

The collection of essays and images gathered here records and pays tribute to the ongoing invention, in work which reaches back over more than three decades, of a consistently challenging professional artist, noted for her collaborations and collisions with a range of artists with whom she has worked and continues to work. At the same time, it is worth pointing out that each of the writers whose work is included has also taken a stand, implicit or explicit, with regard to *knowing the work*, and in this sense the present collection of writing and images takes on a greater challenge: to enquire into knowing itself, in the context of choreographic artistry.

Rosemary Butcher's choreographic and visual art practices have enquired, over the past thirty years, into human *being-in-action,* as that might be portrayed, in quite specific spaces and at different points in time, and in so doing the work has recorded, over the past decades, *something in the air* – which moves and changes. This is a delicate concept, but unavoidable. Its (stubborn) fragility persists, despite the sense that it cannot be readily grasped through mainstream models of representation. Butcher's work goes on challenging, in its refusal to cede to some of the implications of disciplinary convention, even as it draws on the disciplinary mastery – including the expert contribution of other professional artists (whether dancers, lighting designers, composers or film-makers), in performance-designated or other spaces, live or on film – in order to make the work. One of my major preoccupations, in this final essay, will be to try to identify what is brought to Butcher's work by her systematic recourse, within what leans in the direction of a visual arts practice, to the contribution of expert dancers, even today where her new work has begun to shift to the screen. It is this work with dancers, it seems to me, that brings an affective density to the work, together with an engagement with human singularity as well as expertise.

Introduction

It is primarily on the basis of an engagement with her work and its signature, that some of us think that we 'know Rosemary Butcher', the artist. I wonder how well we can know the artist through the work, however, when over a period of decades that same work has seemed to hint at its own secrets, only proceeding then to guard them intact, possibly even from the artist herself.

There is a mystery here, which has a certain appeal. But there is also a challenge to those of us who are writers, and whose task, in part, is to attempt to pin down, to unravel, to unfold, to capture, to expose, to seem to explain, simply *to word*, what the work *might be*; how it manages to appeal to its audiences; how it maintains that appeal over time, while continuing to change and develop. How the work resists – if it resists – the passage of time, when simultaneously it seems to be inflected by, and to wear the marks of the time of its making.

Where might the work seem to *come from*? What were the conditions which might be seen, with the benefit of hindsight, to have enabled it to emerge (if not to have produced it)? How does Butcher sign the work, so that it is recognisably hers, even if that work mostly emerges on the basis of changing collaborations (and collisions) between practising artists from different disciplines? How has it

Butcher's refusal to cede was clear, and it was applauded (if not unambiguously), at The Place, in September 2004, when *Hidden Voices* was shown in London, with Elena Giannotti performing alone, held – trapped? – in a darkened space, bleakly lit, to a sound track from Cathy Lane, and lighting concept by Charles Balfour. The staging seemed to offer almost nothing, in compositional terms, to spectators, trained as many of us are to expect to experience – if only for a moment – that 'Aha!' moment, when hermetic work seems finally to give up what we take to be its secrets. According to Zoe Anderson, writing in *The Independent* (20/9/04) 'Rosemary Butcher's Hidden Voices is a brutal exercise in minimalism... The piece is an endurance test, a point made at exhausting length.' The fact that the piece lasted a mere fifteen minutes sits rather oddly with Anderson's observation.

In compositional terms, what *Hidden Voices* does offer is the almost perfect maintenance, for fifteen minutes, of the same dynamic and kinetic elements we started with. It requires that onlookers – similarly trapped – accept to slow their breathing, watch differently, hold back certain expectations, attending to minuscule change. The piece seems to me, in this sense, to point critically to some of the banal pleasures of rapid change – easier to produce, in dance spaces, than live constancy – which some of us might well take for granted in real-time-based performance. Such a contrast suggests, to me at least, that however much some of us might claim to suffer from (post-)postmodern fatigue, many of us actually treasure what is in fact, in these performance conditions, a wholly conventional moment of insight. Perhaps we do so because it seems, if only for that moment, to admit us into a secret shared with the choreographer or visual artist.

In Butcher's most recent work, I have the clearest sense that secrets exist, and that they are inexhaustible in their implications and complications. As others have indicated in earlier pages, however, such secrets – apparently 'in the work' – may well seem, at times, to have surprised the artist herself, when the work seems to look back at her. In these sorts of terms, even though the possibility of *complicity with the artist* is entertained by the work's intimate relationship with the onlookers, the ('Aha!') moment of apparent complicity with the artist herself is consistently withheld or sidestepped. Perhaps this is because, for Butcher, life itself is unforgiving, barely able, on occasion, to be endured. This insight of mine has come slowly, however, as though in spite of the beauty of the work which has enabled it.

My more general sense is that the conditions of performance themselves are difficult to bear, even though as spectators each of us opts into – and generally pays for as well – the imprisonment entailed. Self-imprisoned in the event, willing 'it' *to work*, I don't simply expect 'something to happen'; instead I seem to require it, not least of the nature of 'event' itself. My need is complex, in the dance-designated space, and it is also curious: it is greater by far than I might experience in a circus tent, when virtuosic action, often performed by an artist *whose name we do not seek out*, seems to suffice. I tend to *make do*, in other words, in the circus tent, with a collective and anonymised naming – 'they...'; 'the performers...' – and in my experience it is rare to wish to identify, in the ring-master, an authorial or signature intervention. I don't, in the circus event, ever

HIDDEN VOICES 2004

6 FRAMES – MEMORIES OF TWO WOMEN
Dublin 2005

suppose, on behalf of that event, that it is required to *do more than it does*, or *show more than it actually shows*. Yet this '*more than*' seems to me to be precisely what some of us ask of 'the choreographer' and of her work with expert dance performers.

Spectators who persist in viewing 'difficult' work in public spaces would seem to have been trained, in the later decades of the 20th century and in the early 21st century, to expect to have to work hard at pleasure. We nonetheless, it seems to me – at least, if we are prepared to sit in silence in curiously constructed spaces, over a period of time, staring ahead of us, and armed only with our expectations – yearn for the sense of a fleeting kind of transcendent communication, between knowing-subjects (amongst whom 'the artist' is the most precious), however fine and momentary that (sensed) communicative experience might be. In the case of Butcher's *Hidden Voices*, such insight comes slowly, and bleakly, with a soft dissipation of energies. A quiet and uninflected 'Ah, I see...' emerged for me, in the event. It came in part from my sense of a breath held, and still held, at the end; from my sense that simple endurance was exceeded – almost unbearably; from my awareness that, in the split second of silence before the applause broke out (the metaphor is apt), something else seemed to me to break, as well. Break softly.

SPACES 4 1981

Part 2

I want at this point to set out and to begin to consider, rather more formally, a question which runs through the essays collected here. It is a question which remains pertinent with regard to Rosemary Butcher's ongoing work, and it is one which seems to me to mark out some of the differences between a choreographic and a visual arts practice. It was triggered, for me, by the role played by Elena Giannotti in *Hidden Voices*, and it emerges, again, in *The Return*, with Eun-Hi-Kim and Martin Otter. It concerns the often unsung artistry of the trained and/or expert dancers who inhabit Butcher's work, and in many senses enable its production; on whose collaborative input that work fundamentally depends, as it comes into being, but who are merely named ('worded') in some of the writing collected in this volume, while remaining 'under erasure', in other essays.

What's in a name? And what remains, when the dancer's name goes under-represented, because it is the choreographer's name which seems to own the work? Perhaps it is the case that the expert input of the named dancer can only be identified in the processes of making the work, whereas the product, or outcome, available to spectator-writers, tends to resonate with a different name? I have found that this sort of question is rarely articulated in writing in the visual arts (including so-called 'arthouse' film).

The aesthetic of *Hidden Voices* depends significantly on the performance qualities and the plasticity of the named dancer herself – the capacity she plainly has to lend herself to, to be impressed into and moulded in terms of, Rosemary Butcher's long-established and ongoing enquiry. The work, after all, taking place in a dance space, was hardly 'dance',

but curiously enough it seemed to me that only the trained and expert dancer could mediate that sense of fragile breakings, of unbearable continuity, which different writers have noted. She alone has the resources permitting her to focus, to intensify, to draw and hold the spectator's look, to command the specular relationship.

In terms of performativity, it was that combination of command and withholding, in the work, which seemed to me to have underlined my sense that the expert choreographer as knowing subject *knows more than she does* (which means that the work resonates 'thickly'), and that she knows differently. It underlines my sense, secondly, that the expert dancer as knowing subject similarly *knows more than she does*, and holds much of that knowing in reserve, as 'expertise' – which means that she is likely to be viewed, professionally, as having considerable professional potential. The same combination enabled me to recognise, in addition, through the work, that Butcher *knows more* (as artist) *than (she can say that) she knows*, for the simplest of reasons, which is that her professional expertise is multi-dimensional, multi-modal, often multi-participant and collaborative, rather than wordable and linear. What this means is that writing, when she herself practises it, will tend to serve and to be secondary to her art, and not vice versa (as is sometimes the case for the work of arts-practitioners entering the university research context, and is the case for the writers gathered in this collection).

In *Hidden Voices* the query established by the work from the outset is sustained beyond the end of the piece – hence, in part, the writerly urge to go on writing. In *The Return* (DVD, 2005, with Martin Otter and Eun-Hi-Kim), the inexhaustible ache of certain images keeps coming back to me, and any sense that it might be released or resolved is effectively undermined first by Butcher's radical avoidance in the work of narrative sequence and linear causality, and second by the state of disciplined *knowing-unknowing* which I have attributed to her.

In compositional terms, the dancer in *Hidden Voices* pulls systematically back from/is pulled back from the energetic follow-through of any gesture, direction or impulse established. As this withholding accumulates, the thematics of (willing self-)imprisonment emerges for me, along with my sense that the potential for meaning-making of a linear kind itself is withheld *over and beyond the period of time available*. In order to stage and embody this undertaking, Giannotti herself needs considerable prudence, considerable expertise, an ability to (agree to) refrain from conventional *expressivity*. (Instead, Butcher *im*-presses.) A further point seems to me to emerge from this account of a dancer's expertise, of her manifest professional judgement (and I want to link this back, once again, to dance-writing and to writing in the visual arts): it is that I am unable, on this sort of basis, to represent Giannotti's own (signature) work by the reductive and objectifying term 'the body' – so widely used in recent years in dance writing and in visual arts writing. Let's suppose, on the contrary, that the somatic complexity of her work is achieved on the basis of considerable expertise and artistry, both of which entail a number of critical instances of, and modes of judgement, including her skill in collaboration.

It might be appropriate, at this point, to begin to enumerate some of the areas in which her own expert judgement is required. As Brian Massumi has pointed out, in another context,[1] the judgement specific to expertise, in the performer, is informed proprioceptively ('defined as the sensibility proper to the muscles and ligaments'), as well as in exteroceptive terms (tactile sensibility) and interoceptive terms ('visceral sensibility'[2]). This is only a starting-point, however, and if we stop here, we run the risk of an apparent re-physicalisation of the dancer's expertise. The 'mature' or professionally trained dancer's expertise-in-action is consistently informed and modulated by her *judgement* – the most difficult quality to separate out from its effects. That judgement is individualised – which is not, however, to say that it is individual, since it is, at the same time, specific to the discipline.

These ways of expert knowing and doing (*in* action) are threaded together, in the growing work, with her ability to interpret, *in* action, the needs of the choreographer; and they are threaded through with her additional capacity to seem to step momentarily out of, and to objectify, her own contribution to the theatricalised, visual complexity. (That stepping-out and auto-reflexive looking is not, however, akin

to the specular activity of the spectator, for the simple reason that the expert dancer also then *steps back in*, to the work, which she modulates). Like many of us in a mediatised culture, the expert dancer has an acute self-gaze, and can be argued to police her own actionally dynamic image. Her expert judgement tends to operate, in the moment (of rehearsal), through an expert sensing and dance-specific intuition and through (expert) feeling, likely to be literalised in/as performance material.

My major point here is that there is *nothing at all*, in either compositional terms, or in terms of the dancer's and the choreographer's expert mastery, of the ready-made, the found object, the banal or the pedestrian, even if it is also the case that Butcher's work, at key historical moments, as a number of writers included here signal, has *thematised* the everyday, its processes and its objects. The pedestrian, after all, as Michel de Certeau's poetic text[3] on the *art of making-do* shows, tends *not to be theatricalised,* as Butcher's objects, persons and processes continue to be*,* for an other's (quasi-public) regard, and to trigger that other's own (aesthetic) judgement, and judgement in terms of signification.

On the other hand, Rosemary Butcher's work has on occasion been positioned in late-modernism, in the postmodern and after it, and over three or more decades it has proceeded through the different feminisms, and responded, in turn, to the outbreak of the very democratic pedestrian arts; it has continued through the fall of the Berlin Wall, to the end of one century and the beginnings – some of them unbearable – of the next. It has 'taken their pulse', as I indicate above, and it resonates – recalling to me the words of the sculptor and visual artist Louise Bourgeois.[4]

Bourgeois, in interview in 1988, talking, one might conclude, 'about her work' (and cited in Stafford[5] in terms of visual analogical practices or connectivities), has observed over a similar period of time what she calls the 'desolation of human relationships' – on which basis her own ethics and aesthetics of practice involve her grouping 'bodies' together, in her installation work, in order to 'see that they touch each other'. 'Touch', here, is metaphoric, as well as literal; it focuses a relation, 'within the work', which expands, then, potentially, to metaphorically touch (and thereby relate to) an

1. B. Massumi, *Parables for the Virtual: Movement, Affect, Sensation,* Duke University Press, Durham and London, 2002, pp.58-59

2. Ibid.

3. M. de Certeau, *The Practice of Everyday Life,* trans. S. Rendall, University of California Press, 1984

4. Louise Bourgeois is a Franco-American artist whose widely ranging work has been linked, historically, with the avant-garde, with feminism, and with psychoanalytic theory (esp. Kleinian theoretical writing) and practices. The most recently published account of her work is M. Nixon's *Fantastic Reality: Louise Bourgeois and the Story of Modern Art,* The MIT Press, Massachusetts and London, 2005.

5. B. M. Stafford, *Visual Analogy: Consciousness as the Art of Connecting,* Massachusetts and London: The MIT Press, 2001 (1999), p.25

SPACES 4 South Bank 1981

SPACES 4 1981

onlooker. In Butcher's work, meanwhile, the sculptural object is replaced by the (expert) human, and the possibility of relating and touching grows literally as well as exponentially. The choreographer must, as a result, understand, contain and modulate the potential to touch, its affective potential; and needs, if this is to be accomplished, expert input from the (named) dancer.

The problem for her as artist, Bourgeois observed, has been 'to put every body in place, to give them a place, and especially to be sure that they are together'.[6] But which body – and whose – do her words refer to? The French philosopher, Gilles Deleuze, writing at the end of the 1960s (around the time when Rosemary Butcher began to make her work), about the 'ethology' of the 17th century philosopher Spinoza,[7] posed a not dissimilar question, pertaining once again, in part, to the ethical and to affectivity:

> How does Spinoza define a body? A body, of whatever kind, is defined in two simultaneous ways. In the first place, a body, however small it may be, is composed of an infinite number of particles; it is the relations of motion and rest, of speeds and slownesses between particles, that define a body, the individuality of a body. Secondly, a body affects other bodies, or is affected by other bodies; it is this capacity for affecting and being affected that also defines a body in its individuality. These two propositions appear to be very simple; one is kinetic and the other, dynamic. (p.123)

6. Bourgeois, quoted ibid.

7. G. Deleuze, *Spinoza: Practical Philosophy,* trans. R.Hurley, San Francisco: City Lights Books, 1988 (first published in the French as *Spinoza: Philosophie pratique*, Presses Universitaires de France, 1970)

8. B. Massumi, *Parables for the Virtual: Movement, Affect, Sensation,* Duke University Press, Durham and London, 2002

9. Ibid.

10. Traditionally, ethology is concerned with animal behaviour, and the attempt to formalise observation and description; but ethology includes studies of instinct, more generally, and the attempt to relate *behaviour observed* to cognitive function. Hence the connection with the work of Rudolf Laban is clear.

178

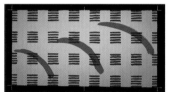

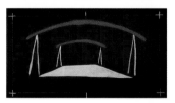

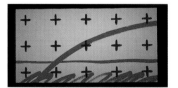

d1, d2, & 3D 1990
this page: Designs by John Lyall

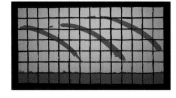

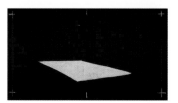

d2 1990

Part 3   We need to avoid literalising 'a body', in this context, since in Deleuze's reconfigured 'Spinoza…', that body might be animal or plant life, scientifically observed; in Bourgeois's work it might be mineral, certainly material, analytically, syncretically and aesthetically observed and positioned. In Butcher's work, which takes the singular plasticity and actional potential of certain expert dancers as its compositional *focus*, 'body' is both literal and metaphoric, and the word itself is inadequate.

Even when it is literalised in choreographic practice – *'her expert dancer's* body' – that *expert* 'bodyness' has only a passing 'thingness', in contrast with what might be suggested by the term 'the body'. Instead, as Deleuze's writing enables me to suggest, what a dancer makes available to choreography is *particulate*, mediated by energy production and use, rather more than it is solid or hard-edged, or monolithic. The expert dancer is gifted in this offering of potential – and aspires, in turn, to qualitative transformation. In these terms, this expert bodywork is both given (in part), and it is emergent (despite its individual,

professional history), rather than given as such. Its operations are fleeting, while its particles are momentarily stabilised, coalesce, are theatricalised (by which I mean, in part, that they are made available to be looked at twice).

What the collaborating expert dancers at work with the choreographer might also be enabled to articulate, and what is articulated as though 'across' her or him, is patently not akin to, nor is it commensurable with, either her or his everyday body (which expertise and choreography transform), or (despite the claims of the 'textual turn' of the later 20th century), with *text*.

In/as elements within 'the work', in which the particles from which spectators constitute Butcher's signature flicker, the performer's expertise and artistry is more than three times invested: first, by each dancer's own creative as well as professional aspiration (to what Brian Massumi has called 'qualitative transformation'[8]) and her or his affective investment in it; second, by Butcher's investment, which is existential, as well as creative and epistemic (or knowledge-centred and internally varying); third by what is pressed into them by spectators, by spectators' expectations, and by the nature of 'event' itself. These different investments can be identified in terms of different process threads,[9] and to some extent they can be separated out artificially, because language permits us to name them (if not, in so doing, to grasp their full complexities); whereas 'the work' tends to draw them together syncretically, and to weave with them. In each of these different investments, bound together as performance, the Spinozan impress, as Deleuze has rearticulated it, can be identified.

To summarise my central argument here: Rosemary Butcher's insistence that she make new work with expert, trained dancers, whose artistry and disciplinary mastery she can take as a starting-point in a collaborative composition, means that she grants herself the opportunity to explore, with each, the Spinozan 'infinite number of particles, …relations of motion and rest, of speeds and slownesses between particles', as well as 'this capacity for affecting and being affected that also defines a body in its individuality'.

Given the broad interpretation of ethology,[10] which I have brought via Deleuze into this framework, it is this concern for individuality which I want to emphasise here: the individuality of expert, named dancers, their maturity, grasp of performance-making, the repertoire of options they can make available to the generation of new material, their resilience and their circumspection – as well as their individual 'look' and way of being in space and time – are consistently profiled in Rosemary Butcher's 'science', even when she thematises the everyday; so, too, in rather more determinate terms, is that expert dancer's capacity for judgement in action.

d1, d2, & 3D 1990
this page: Designs by John Lyall

Part 4   What does it mean to argue, tentatively, that Butcher's ongoing enquiry (if not any one of the individual works itself) is ethological? That she has been concerned throughout with exploring, in given socio-cultural and dance-specific contexts and situations, in response to creative as well as professional and philosophical 'imperatives', possible relations established between (expert and singular) bodies, for the sustained look of an other? Can we begin to argue, on the basis of the work itself (which 'work' necessarily includes every professional 'thing' that can be inferred from, but is not visible as such 'in the piece' – such as casting, collaboration, workshop and rehearsal) that Butcher is a dance scientist? Plainly the work does not expound its scientific status in the sorts of expert registers used by professional researchers in the university, who seek to specify discursively the links between motion and emotion;[11] but the audience reached, in Butcher's case, is almost certainly broader, and likely – on the basis of that sustained look which dance events address – to be differently affected. Let's make no mistake as to the epistemic (or knowledge-centred) nature of Butcher's enquiry: the Spinozan ethology, as Deleuze pointed out in the early 1970s, involves – as does Butcher's – a 'long affair of experimentation, requiring a lasting prudence'. It is precisely 'because no one knows ahead of time the affects [on other bodies] one is capable of' (125), in changing situations and contexts, that Butcher's work continues its enquiry.

Butcher, in the terms I have set out above, *is fully familiar with the processes of systematic and ongoing enquiry* (of which casting, collaboration, 'the workshop', and 'the rehearsal', constitute four examples) that allow her not simply to arrive at the production of 'challenging' new work, but to believe in that capacity in herself. The works themselves reveal a range of imperatives, and investments, which are consistently articulated together with that ongoing enquiry, as well as that belief; yet she makes no claim whatsoever as to the usefulness, to the artist's ongoing productivity, of that type of dance-ethological knowledge which takes writing as its principal articulation – and indeed she has no need to. It is by the work and its signature, its often observed 'difficulty', but also its ethics of collaborative practice, that so many of us know her.

I want to test the Deleuzian observation once more against Butcher's own practices, before I proceed to introduce the other writers' work assembled here. The Spinozan 'ethics', Deleuze goes on, 'has nothing to do with a morality; he conceives it... as a composition of fast and slow speeds, of capacities for affecting and being affected on [the] plane of immanence'. With reference then to Rosemary Butcher's work: this work has nothing to do with a morality. She approaches it, in significant part, as a creative-ethological experiment in contemporary visual and human action-based aesthetics, drawing on the input of expert, named dancers (and other collaborators), to produce a new composition of fast and slow speeds, of capacities for affecting and being affected, on the plane of immanence of (hence recognisable in disciplinary terms as) 'dance performance'. The work emerges through a long affair of experimentation, requiring a lasting prudence, because the choreographic artist does not know, ahead of time, the affects, on other bodies (including those of spectators, but also of film-maker, sound designer and lighting designer), that her work is capable of summoning forth.

In the most recent work, Butcher explores the transfer to film of dance's performance specificity, which she thereby *theorises in/as expert multidimensional action,* 'reduced' and intensified through recourse to filmic registers. Butcher works in particular, with the camera in mind, with the trained dancer's upper torso, arms, hands and face: she choreographs and films faciality itself, seemingly seeking to reveal 'something', which emerges *over time,* not in an instant, and in filigree. Hence what is, or might be, revealed, is not of the immediate surface – yet paradoxically the surface is its site; to identify it, where it appears, those of us who spectate need a founding story about human complexity, a relation to the exterior perceived, of one or another story of interiorities.

The work emerges through a sustained, choreographic observation of tiny, particulate movement, tiny particulate changes[12] in the visual, perceived in the rehearsal space, which a particular expert dancer (and not others), watched intently, and called upon, can make (always imperfectly) available. What I find in Butcher's later work is a curious mode of dynamic-kinetic portraiture, eminently realisable on film or video, but rarely undertaken by film-makers or video artists themselves, who tend to prefer the dynamic of narrative characterisation, visible interaction, a relation (enacted) to situation and 'world'. Butcher chooses the faces and hands and upper torso of expert dance practitioners, who are accustomed to work with the choreographic requirement that *something* (seem to) *be revealed somatically*. Butcher seems to me to aim, in these terms, for what Lagneau, quoted in Deleuze's *Spinoza...*, has described as a 'capacity for discerning in a single act the relationship of the greatest possible number of thoughts'.[13]

11. The study of the links between motion and emotion was formalised, in terms of dance at least, in the modernist dance-analytic programme deriving from the work of Rudolf Laban.

12. 'Particulate', because they operate at a finer level than is understood by the order of 'the sign'. These are not 'signs', but rather the flickering that one or another viewer will gather and combine, on which basis s/he will semiotise what she has herself brought into meaningful 'being'; and in my experience, she will argue, then, that these were 'already there'.

13. G. Deleuze, *Spinoza: Practical Philosophy,* trans. R.Hurley, San Francisco: City Lights Books, 1988, p. 127

Part 5 How might the expertise of the artist be viewed in academic contexts which focus on creative and performing arts, but largely from the positions and presuppositions of an expert spectating – a spectating which also takes the production of writing as its primary objective? I have suggested that choreographic practices and expertise operate in a radical outside of writing, meaning that there is no easy 'fit' between the former and the latter. I have gone further, in order to suggest that the expert choreographer *thinks* (in expert practice) *geometrically, diagrammatically, schematically, and multi-dimensional*y, rather than in the linear-dominant mode bound-in to writing.

It is on this sort of basis that I have argued that there are questions of knowledge (of causes, of contexts, of situations, of actions, of artists...) at stake here, and that they reach beyond 'the work itself', to encompass *the person* of the arts professional. What Deleuze noted in his *Spinoza...* is that a philosopher's life – and, I would add, a professional artist's life – has a particular mystery to it. He sets out some of the terms of that mystery as follows: the 'philosopher [or artist] appropriates the ascetic virtues – humility, poverty, [if not necessarily] chastity – and makes them serve ends completely [her] own, extraordinary ends that are not very ascetic at all, in fact'.[14] They are not very ascetic at all, he argues, in the sense that this life which might appear to be one of lack, is actually 'a life no longer lived... in terms of means and ends, but according to a production, a productivity, a potency'. Rosemary Butcher's life, at least from where I view it, is lived according to 'a production, a productivity, a potency', marked by her signature (or graphic trace).

Butcher's work, however, is not in fact concerned with 'a body', as a philosophical *text* might be, nor even with 'some body'. Philosophical *writing* tends to generalise, even when its concern is the singular. I have indicated that it is not possible to generalise choreographic specificity, not least where a named practitioner's work is at stake. If Butcher's work is intimately and consistently concerned with, and composed in terms of, what Deleuze calls the 'relations of motion and rest, of speeds and slownesses between particles, that define a body, the individuality of a body', it is vital to differentiate between *what* choreographic

14. G. Deleuze, *Spinoza: Practical Philosophy,* trans. R.Hurley, San Francisco: City Lights Books, 1988, p. 127

NIGHT MOORING STONES 1984
Prep work, Dundee

practice can *thematise*, *how* it does so, and how that doing and its thematisations *differ* from those of writing. Denying this constitutive difference is either lazy, or that denial practises a colonisation by writing of writing's radical other. Writing, besides, is one of the most conventional and rule-governed practices we have available, even if what it can thematise seems to be infinite.

If Butcher's work, then, has plainly been concerned both with 'the individuality of a body', which that work systematically thematises, and with staging the possible relations between bodies – such as we saw in Louise Bourgeois' observations briefly cited above – it is also the case that the *way* Butcher *makes work*, is singular, signature-specific, but recognisably 'dance'. It engages not with 'a body', nor with the universal 'any body', but rather with '*this* [named, expert dancer's] body[work]', displayed to an other's sustained look. Whereas Butcher's expert art practices *thematise* concerns familiar from philosophical writing, to bring this about, Butcher must draw on the expert or disciplinary, named dancer as real, as singular, as symbol, and as a constitutive element in the dance symbolic.

Here lies a key difference between the *economy of the text*, to which Susan Leigh Foster refers in the present volume, the place of reading or writing in that economy, on the one hand, and on the other expert performance-making in the specular and event-specific economies. In place of the clause, the paragraph, or the text (or indeed the intertext), Butcher's own philosophical engagement, which is always also an experiment in aesthetic terms, challenges too in compositional terms. It is *other than syntactic* in its performative engagement. There is no equivalence between the order of the well-behaved text, in the economy of writing, and the choreographic experiment that is new dance, or dance on screen, professionally produced.

Hence when Butcher's work reveals, as it certainly does, that 'a body affects other bodies, or is affected by other bodies', it does so, in addition, on the basis of the acutely performance-determining qualities of a particular named dancer's expertise, her contribution, and her own work's emergent qualities. While I have constantly to seem, as writer, to negotiate *with traditions of writing* the words I put together, the key difference between Butcher's expertise and mine is that the words I choose are also mine (and yours), whereas 'Butcher's dancers' (as I so easily qualify them) are not, in fact, hers. They are not merely her other, but first, that otherness is constitutive of her aesthetic signature; and second, the dancers themselves are also the promise of a qualitative transformation that will, in the best of cases, surprise both of them.

Now, *if* we can accept that Rosemary Butcher philosophises in *and as* choreographic action, drawing on the artistry of a whole range of expert practitioners in order to produce choreographic practices which are dense, 'thick' in their rich evocation, but at the same time minimalist, speculative, resonant, and elusive, we need to be clearer with regard to the ways in which this philosophical undertaking works. My own suggestion is that this sort of density and complexity engages spectators and listeners – *when it works* – in the productive operations of catalysis, as well as hypotyposis. Catalysis means that the whole is more than the sum of its parts, because each functions to transform its other. Hypotyposis, meanwhile, involves a highly economical, vivid sketch or outline – either visual, movement-based or sonoric, or all of these – which operates in the given economy of (art) production by enabling a listener or spectator to perceive *as present* something complex which, by definition, cannot be present/ed, because it operates below the levels of sensory representation.[15] On this basis I am going to proceed to argue that Rosemary Butcher *philosophises* multi-dimensionally, with considerable economy, through multi-schematic and multi-participant, *signed* arts practice, with qualitative transformation in mind, by requiring of her spectators that we provide what she does not, but in terms which she has conditioned.

Others have noted that Rosemary Butcher's ways of seeing and doing tend toward the geometric, the architectural, the associative, the speculative and, in addition, the poetic, humanist and expressive. Her philosophical practices, in other words, rather than 'writing-like', instead enact and instantiate a 'something (schematic and symbolic)', which triggers in some spectators at least their own productive input. This 'something' is *im*-pressed in multi-dimensional mode, into the (expert) human real, both

by choreography, and by spectating.

In so doing, rather than generalising, Butcher's practices singularise, ostending this or that particular, named dancer-artist at work under her impress; that dancer's particular height, body mass, musculature, faciality, gestuality, way of moving and of not moving; ethnicity; gender; her or his colouring, her or his look (or plasticity). This recourse to the real human, which we can only engage with, as spectators, on the basis of Butcher's compositional choices, invites viewers themselves to move from the minimal to the extensive; from the exemplary, the singular, and the particular, *to* the general – whereas writing-bound philosophical practices tend to encourage us to move in the opposite direction. In so doing, they tend to profile and to prioritise the operations and outcome of *expert or professional intuition*, which the professional artist tends to sense, rather than to 'think' (I am supposing that there are differences here, in brain site, and in type of brain activity), proceeding to subject these, in discipline-specific manner, to the logics of production and professional production values.

Plainly there is nothing new in intuitive processes, which have been investigated in mainstream philosophical writing ranging from Descartes to Kant and, more recently, Deleuze, as well as in writing on education and creativity. The processes which interest me are not simply intuitive, however. Instead, when I am confronted by Rosemary Butcher's work, I am concerned with *the operation of 'expert or professional intuitive processes'*, brought into productive interface with the logics of performance production and its event. For some readers, the notion of expert intuition might recall aspects of the Kantian philosophical concern with what have been called 'sensible intuitions'. Sensible intuitions, in the case of expert practices, are not static, and self-defined or defining, as may be the case with some of our everyday intuitions. Instead, they participate in the generation of aesthetic practices and/or objects; in certain instances of Rosemary Butcher's work – and this is the case for *Hidden Voices*, and for *The Return* – these expert intuitions, in the practitioner, will tend to trigger other intuitions, in the expert spectator. That spectator will seem, in turn, to grasp through them the capacity, 'for discerning in a single act [of performance] the relationship of the greatest possible number of thoughts'.[16]

Sensible intuitions (which seem to spring from a nowhere of rational thought), operate, in choreographic practice, alongside elements which can only be *thought* (the latter involve, for example, the logics of production and interpretation, also brought to the making processes by the choreographer), according to what the Kantian tradition has called 'symbolic exhibition'. Symbolic exhibition is given as one aspect of the rhetorical function of hypotyposis.

15. 'Hypotyposis', traceable back to the Ancient Greek, is identified by Paul de Man in terms of a figuration, 'which makes present, to the senses, something which is out of their reach, not just because it does not happen to be there but because it consists, in whole or in part, of elements too abstract for sensory representation'. See Paul de Man, in Sheldon Sacks (ed.) *On Metaphor*, University of Chicago Press, 1979.

16. J. Lagneau, *Célèbres leçons et fragments*, P.U.F. 1964, cited in G. Deleuze, *Spinoza: Practical Philosophy*, trans. R.Hurley, San Francisco: City Lights Books, 1988.

NIGHT MOORING STONES 1984

Because they are identified as 'too abstract for sensory representation', such performance 'elements' seem to operate 'below' the level of 'the sign' – a crude conceptual mechanism still introduced to undergraduates as one element in performance analysis, from the perspective of the spectator. In these sorts of terms, these particles are 'subsemiotic', and they flicker apparently across 'a work', while contributing significantly to the sense we get of that work – *if* we are prepared to work with it in its own terms. In the rehearsal circumstances, the 'sensible intuition' emerges in part in response to contingent factors – the sudden angle, and power of revelation, of a bar of sunlight, through the studio window; the haze of dust through which the light flickers, and falls; the sudden weight of a body held, seen from here... or here... or there; the chance co-incidence of recorded sound and breath held.

Rosemary Butcher's complex and minimalist 'figuring', in *Hidden Voices* and in *The Return* – but radically different in each of these – works in such a way as to offer more than it actually gives, despite the sense I get, as spectator, that it has given more; that what I get, I get 'from it' (the gift, in terms of Heidegger's philosophical writing, requires very little of me in return – hence the apparent frugality of the professional artist's life). The minute detail of the so-called 'pre-' or 'sub-semiotic' figuring seems to be scattered across the available choreographic options, and to be in repose in none of these. It is catalytic, in the sense that this minutely detailed ordering is internally productive and transformative. In the latter sense, what we observe can only be understood, in disciplinary and compositional terms, on the basis of the *intertwining* the artist will have effected, by adding heat to it, between the stuff of sensible intuition and what can only be thought *and subjected to disciplinary and personal judgement*, which also orders it.

Symbolic exhibition in Butcher's work, then, emerges on the basis of the transfer of sensible (expert) intuitions, in major or minor keys, into concrete practices, made available to spectators. As far as I have been able to tell, the expert choreographer achieves this transfer by bringing to them both her own conceptual signature, and the operations specific to a set of disciplinary rules. The disciplinary rules are not however wholly able to determine the new work: if they could, it would be judged to be repetitive or derivative. The discipline-specific rules seem to enable the artist to make a new concept available to the work, effectively to reveal a new rule, which the broader discipline itself will in turn expand, in certain instances, to take up. In Rosemary Butcher's case, we can see the work of this set of disciplinary rules, and the production values they involve, on the basis of which her still-growing national and international reputation is grounded. Her ways of seeing and doing, her ways of knowing, have gone (as algorithm) into, and they expand, the visual arts as well as the choreographic repertoire.

At work in the rehearsal space with a dancer, when the work is 'going well', it seems to me that Rosemary Butcher's interventions work to establish the possibility of her effecting a concrete analogy – compositional, at its most basic; possibly visual; possibly relational (between bodies, and gazes); possibly all of these, but equally actional, tactile, haptic – with the materials available, 'in which [her] judgment performs a double function'.[17] Such an analogy, Stafford has recently argued, in terms which are respectful of the artist's ongoing affective (indeed existential) drive to make new work,[18] is 'born of a human desire to achieve union with that which one does not possess'. It also entails, Stafford adds, 'a passionate process marked by fluid oscillations', involving the (Lacanian[19]) quest for 'an approximating resemblance', possibly diagrammatic or schematic, rather than mimetic, which might momentarily seem ' to fill [the] place' of 'that which one does not possess' (2).

First, Rosemary Butcher brings to this choreographic task and to the intuitions it excites, the *conceptual order* which she has developed through the history of her dance-making, and which bears her signature: she makes the emergent her own. Second, she reflects on sensible intuitions through her bringing to them the conceptual order specific to her own highly individual ways of seeing. She juggles these. Third, she brings disciplinary rules and production values – choreographic, visual art-specific – to bear on them. Fourth, she reviews this combination, and the thematic values which begin to emerge, in terms of the as-yet scarcely imaginable 'new work', to which she is professionally committed, and which will have, in terms of her own judgement and exigency, to be qualitatively transformed, to surprise her, while bearing her signature.

It is at the interface her work establishes between these aspects – the signed and singular conceptual, the disciplinary and rule-governed, the 'pulse-taking' specific to a given time and place – that rehearsal observers begin to see the emergence of 'something new', an instance of symbolic exhibition, in which the particular emergent qualities of the dancer as artist play a key role. Next, she modulates this emerging complexity, its density, its human-expressive and evocative power, by beginning to weave into it those process threads [20] and that positioning, which together articulate the drive that informs the practices: to make new work, which will look back at her.

If the sensible intuition appears to the senses as though in a flash, seeming to come from nowhere, yet it comes, it would appear, from a new and highly specific patterning of the complex mass of acquired, expert, overlayered experience and perception of the artist herself. It cannot be commanded forth, although 'the professional' depends upon its emergence. It is on this basis that the workshop or rehearsal needs to be identified in terms of a stabilised experimental environment. When it emerges, in the arts-professional context, the intuition also tends to do so on the basis of a particular objective or objectives in view – for example, a specific professional production date, as well as an affectively informed and a qualitatively transforming objective. In this sense what emerges will already be heavy with past, present and future perspectives. Butcher captures it, in its fragility and uncertainty. She overlays that fragile material with the *rules* (specific to choreographic production) which she has mastered over a lifetime's work, and with a different future (new work) in view. In so doing, she also reflects on that intuition, retaining and discarding some of its implications; and she proceeds then to apply the merging of concept, intuition, and rule to an entirely different, signed, (philosophical) object – still called 'dance'.

I have argued elsewhere,[21] on the issue of the operation of expert intuition, that some of the most notorious theoretical writers, over the final decades of the 20th century, whose writing is found to be particularly interesting by those involved in the visual and performance arts, have themselves used expert intuition whenever they have found themselves preoccupied with the task of theorising the radical outside of writing. The challenge that this 'radical outside' brings to philosophy, according to the cognitive neuroscientist, Steven Pinker,[22] lies in its quality as 'something [that is] peculiarly holistic and everywhere-at-once and nowhere-at-all and all-at-the-same-time'. Its complexities are such as to test even the greatest 'compositional [and] combinatorial abilities' (140)[23] of the human mind. In her highly particular aesthetic, Rosemary Butcher chooses expert choreographic and filmic practices as the preferred means to articulate her own speculative and constantly reappraised grasp of these complexities.

17. Kant's *Critique of Judgement*, trans. with editorial notes by Werner S. Pluhar, Indianapolis and Cambridge, Massachusetts: Hackett Publishing Company, 1987

18. B. M. Stafford, *Visual Analogy: Consciousness as the Art of Connecting*, Massachusetts and London: The MIT Press, 2001 (1999)

19. The Lacanian psychoanalytic tradition (although she does not otherwise invoke it) provides B. Stafford, as it does many other writers concerned with art practices, with the notion of the 'game of back and forth' (*Fort/Da!*), with which she begins her study of visual analogy. See, for example, J. Lacan, *Ecrits: A Selection*, trans. A. Sheridan, London: Tavistock Publications, 1977.

20. B. Massumi, *Parables for the Virtual: Movement, Affect, Sensation*, Durham & London: Duke University Press, 2002

21. http://www.sfmelrose.u-net.com/justintuitive

22. Steven Pinker, *The Blank Slate: the Modern Denial of Human Nature*, London: Allen Lane (Penguin Press), 2002, p.564

23. Ibid. p.120

GROUND LINE
Arnolfini 1976

Conclusion I have sought, in these final pages, to do something quite specific: that is, to underline my assertion that the various instances of writing included in the present study together frame Rosemary Butcher's expert practices in such a way as to reveal within them an ongoing, unresolved, philosophical as well as epistemic (or knowledge-centred, research) engagement. My final question, in these terms, is simple: what precisely can one enquire into, in philosophical terms, choreographically? In this particular case, the philosophical engagement weaves together a particular aesthetic; a number of ways of knowing, hence a *techne* – or craft, or way of expert-doing (that is, a practice grounded in an 'account' – something involving theoretical understanding).[24] That techne, or a way of expert or professional knowing and doing, is itself informed – in this particular case – by the choreographer's own wider and constantly shifting knowledge of contemporary art practices. From this perspective, Rosemary Butcher's engagement in pursuing her own creative practices is also that of an expert (art) witness, whose own practices engage with and account – in speculative and reflexive mode – for aspects of the changing visual art context and choreographic contexts, within which she has found herself at work, over the past three decades. This is a remarkable achievement.

24. For a very useful account of the relationship between techne and episteme, before Aristotelian intervention, see R. Parry, '*Episteme* and *Techne*', *The Stanford Encyclopedia of Philosophy (Summer 2003 Edition)*, Edward N. Zalta (ed.), http://plato.stanford.edu/archives/sum2003/entries/episteme-techne.

CATCH FIVE CATCH SIX 1978

DANCES FOR DIFFERENT SPACES
Florence 1978

DANCES FOR DIFFERENT SPACES
Chiswick House, London, 1978

DANCES FOR DIFFERENT SPACES
Museum of Modern Art, Oxford

FIELD BEYOND THE MAPS
Prep work, Riverside Studios roof, London, 1979

AFTERWORD: BACKWARD GLANCES, 1971-2000

A conversation with Rosemary Butcher

I got into Dartington because I was viewed to have a certain quality, but I had no technique. I wafted in the garden while my mother played the piano. In the first visit to New York I went to the Martha Graham Studio, and then in the second I was with artists like Merce Cunningham, Trisha Brown, Yvonne Rainer, Lucinda Childs and Meredith Monk, and I went to everything that was on. Film was very important – Godard, Bunuel, Andy Warhol's films. I came back to the UK for a holiday, having decided that I'd live in New York, but then I couldn't go back because my visa was cancelled. I got a job at the Scottish Theatre Ballet, a modern dance company, as a teacher and trainer. I made a piece for them to tour, called **Uneven Time** (1973) which was reviewed in the Scottish press. That was a complete breakthrough technically for me. I'd changed pieces overnight previously – when I saw Cunningham, for instance. I had been trained very tightly in Graham Technique, and all I knew was the body; but when I moved on I didn't know what I wanted to produce, but I knew quite clearly that I didn't want to do that. There'd been a definite self-satisfaction about the Graham technique, and there was very little need to do anything other than that. But there was a real problem in my thinking: I'd realised that dance could be absolutely *anything*. It was like a door had opened for me onto some kind of revelation. I didn't realise it at the time but here was a conceptual movement, where you could get rid of – all that [dance] *stuff,* that to me didn't have anything to do with the Idea. It was like I was two different people – if I had had any other craft, then I wouldn't have ended up with dance…

To me, dance was pushing me away from something that needed to be said. It was always a conflict – I couldn't reconcile the passivity of a still body [in dance in the 1970s] as being a resolution of an idea. It's different now because there has been a whole movement that I feel very associated with, where the body in art has become very strong, in work by artists who haven't been dancers – a whole group of artists where the body has been absolutely central to what they've been making. They haven't *choreographed* these bodies. But most of the work I responded to in New York didn't have form at its centre; form was not… whatever it *was*, it wasn't artefact, and it didn't have a formal aesthetic that I responded to. I responded to the minds of these people – that was the great thing. These people were extremely exacting, workshops enquiring very deeply into the choreographic level of the voice, for example, or the site. It took me ten years to leave [the dance training], and I still felt that I hadn't got anywhere. I don't know if that was a good thing or a bad thing. At least the skills training allowed other things to come through…

Most of the work that interested me wasn't something that I could re-do in dance. What it was about was the experience of a moment, or seeing someone experiencing a moment, enabled by someone else. The inspiration is non-definable, because *something happens*, which is not to do with understanding, it's to do with seeing something going on. What kept drawing me back wasn't knowledge or technique, it was philosophical; but I don't get that experience from dance. And I haven't got it from dance since the 1970s when I saw Merce Cunningham, early Lucinda Childs, *Walking on the Walls* by Trisha Brown, *Turtle Dreams* by Meredith Monk, *Einstein on the Beach* by Robert Wilson, *Dr Faustus Lights the Lights*, and some of Peter Brook's

theatre work. I was very attracted very early on to Wilson's work. It was very broken down, it had no development at all, and then it got very obscure, and more and more extraordinary – the light, and the sound, and the magic. I'd never seen anything like it.

Passage North East (1976) was an outside piece, made at the Arnolfini, in Bristol, with dancers on one side of the water, in a disused warehouse, and they were very small, and then a boat picked them up, and then they came very close up. This was very much influenced by the Staten Island ferry work of the Sneaker Brigade, in New York. What was interesting about this was not the movement, but the space, and the space between the movements. When I look back at it now, on film, the dancers are still fantastic, but my choreography is very strange, it looks so improvised, but what was important was the idea of six people in white, moving simultaneously – in other words I was working with the concept of what was happening. It was contact improvisation taken completely out of its own context and put into my context. Bridget Riley's painting was particularly influential here. Space was mapped out for me in her work – squares, lines, colours, textures, light, and I evidently was already thinking, how can I put that into… It wasn't a matter of how that texture might be, in dance technical terms, and it wasn't interpretative.

The piece was entirely based on lines that were parallel, on the diagonal. It was about structures, that gave me something that held the work in a frame – a grid, which enabled me to see something… I realise now that it was abstract. I didn't set a grid up, but it emerged, from the questions I asked [the dancers]. I was trying to get rid of something human, but I wasn't [getting rid of it]. I am still very attached to line, to precision, but now my goals are very different. It was hugely satisfying to have resolved it, and I did feel that I was coming to understand something, every time I got through these processes, something about me. Then it enabled me to cope with other things. Without it, there was an absolute void, as to the point of anything. Other people saw something there. And otherwise I didn't know how I would live. But I didn't have this sort of explanation at the time. All I do know is that what that sort of work did do, at the time, was usher in the alternative movement, the letting go of the psyche, and that was the confusion, because psychologically, this alternative work said 'Let's let everything go! Let's let dance be anything!' There was a feel-good factor: 'Anyone can dance!' and at the same time these ideas were running alongside the work; but what was problematic with this breaking through from the world of technique was the question of whether what was made could actually be accepted as an art form. Most of the criticisms through this whole period were that the work was 'so badly danced'. These pieces refused conventional style, but they were influenced then by what other people saw as alternative beings, who in terms of the work were actually highly trained dancers. My whole thing, as a trainer, was to de-train them, but what people *saw* at the same time was a new style, which was called the alternative movement.

The London Contemporary Dance Company was in its early years, when I was making the late 1970s work, so by then this challenge had turned into 'contemporary dance'. In **White Field** (1977), at the Riverside Studios, I was dealing with real time, something I'd picked up from film. And I started working on collaborations, *with* different artists, instead of being influenced by other artists. I made five pieces eventually with the sculptor, Heinz Dieter Pietsch – we pushed each other. We moved into light, into sculpture, into making opportunities for this work to be set against another work or space, which brought

1971-73
New York

1976-77
The Serpentine Gallery, London

1973-76
The Arnolfini Gallery, Bristol
Riverside Studios, London

with it another context. A lot of the preparation was done in the [London] Docklands area, which provided a lot of the inspiration. A lot of influence came from the wasteland of the Docklands themselves. Other artists came in from other fields, with their own painting and sculpture, as well as what were then to me new technologies. **The Site** and **Imprints**, both (1983), were very important. **The Site** was an archaeological dig, and it was the most experimental of all the pieces I was making. The inspiration was a Saxon fort, and there was wind and the atmosphere of the wildness, but that piece was looking at what was underground, and what was above ground. I took the metaphor of the site, and the post holes, so there was a notion of something underpinning – the movement of the dancers was as though there was something underpinning them. So everything seemed to be turned inside out, and it looked then like we were looking at it from underneath, and at an angle. Philosophically, it was very complex, and it was delivered with four neon strips, placed in a grid. The lighting was by Dieter Pietsch – and the dancers hung over the neon strips, which lit them from below.

Around this time I was working with improvisation and with particular gifted dancers at the Riverside. We were really lucky – I was resident for two years when there were all these wonderful things happening – Samuel Beckett came, Geraldine Chaplin and *Le Cercle Magique,* Hanif Kureishi was around; Will Allsop and John Lyall had their offices there, and they designed the bookshop. I had the little old Sound Room, as my studio. The actual atmosphere at the Riverside at its height had a huge influence on me. Peter Gill was resident director, and they brought over a lot of international artists, and we saw some very interesting modern work in dance – Lucinda Child's *Diagonal Pieces*, with Sol LeWitt; Trisha Brown's *Set and Reset*, with the video projected up above it. These were Riverside landmarks for me. This time had a huge influence on me – and for me it was probably quite dance-influenced, not exactly by the work itself, but the backgrounds of those people. The great thing was that I got free studio space and I taught once a week. At that time, David Gothard at the Riverside supported the work of theatre and dance rebels when the Arts Council didn't. I made **Night Mooring Stones** (1984) with the film-maker, Jane Rigby and the composer Max Eastly, and Gaby Agis, Helen Rowsell and Dennis Greenwood – and Channel 4 picked it up for SPACES 4 [on television] in the same year.

Over that same period there was the Dartington Festival, but it didn't have much impact on London. It involved thirteen years of bringing over really important international artists – the descendants of people like Trisha Brown. But they didn't ever come to London in all that time. There is a very interesting unwritten history here – a history of the influence of Dartington. My work had already been influenced by Dartington, so the effect was there even so...

I had a ten-year retrospective, **Ten Years On**, in 1986 at Riverside. I included **Flying Lines** – the most dance-based piece I ever made, with eight dancers, and it was very much influenced by kite flying. It was the beginning of the emergence of the functional guide – How to do… something, guides, and manuals – and it was a time when people were wondering why other people flew kites. And it seemed to be because it was a way of lifting oneself out of the everyday.

Touch the Earth (1987) was a large-scale piece – I went from very intimate pieces to very large scale. **Flying Lines**, **Touch the Earth**, **After the Crying and the Shouting** (1989), **d1, d2, 3D** (1989-1990) and **Of Shadows and Walls** (1991) were all collaborations with numbers and objects which seemed to come – I don't actually know

where this was coming from. Maybe it was the influence of theatre – I think that the scale of the work and the sense of putting something together was possibly about my trying to engage in theatre-making. It was about a group, group energy. I had started to visit architectural sites with Nigel [Butcher]. He took me to visit some of the major architectural icons of the twentieth century, looking for example at Corbusier's work, and at work which theatricalises the space, at amazing buildings constructed into space, lit extraordinarily by real light, or where the whole building was built on a grid. I began to visit architectural sites like *Unité d'Habitation* in Marseille, constructed within particular spaces – and the feeling of being in those buildings, those spaces, stayed in my mind. I was to use Le Corbusier's Modric (a system he devised for measurement and proportion which I saw etched into the floor at his pilgrimage chapel Ronchamp) for the structure of the '*Ds*'.

Touch the Earth was influenced by McLuhan's book, *Touch the Earth: Self-portrait of an Indian Existence* [1972; Abacus 1987] about American indigenous people having no home. Pictures were taken of that time when they were in exile, and Dieter found all sorts of connections with agricultural tools. He built abstract objects to do with tents. The work was getting quite narrative in focus, and **Touch the Earth** in particular was extremely well received.

For **After the Crying and the Shouting** (1989) I used a piece of music written by Wim Mertens, but it wasn't a collaboration. He was part of that group of contemporary composers who were interested in systems, and grids – and really at this time the principal influence was music. But then I went right back into architecture for **d1**, **d2**, **3D** (1989-1990). I wanted to pull all of the earlier work with space together. I decided that I'd make a piece that was made first for one space, and then elaborated for another space, and then re-elaborated for a third space. It grew every time it moved, and we took a series of different venues, so we were looking at a sort of site-specific inspiration, starting at the Royal Festival Hall. Zaha Hadid was the architect for **d1**. She made wonderful designs on the floor, and we had long, long conversations, but finally we found it very difficult to collaborate and it didn't really happen. Her more recent collaborations have effectively involved a [theatrical] set, with furniture, and big, big design, whereas I had wanted something more subtle. The ideas had been wonderful – ley lines [alignments of ancient sites stretching across the landscape] and a construct built from lines, in different dimensions. Then the architect John Lyall worked with me on **d2** and **3D**, in Scotland. It was only staged once, at the Tramway. It would be wonderful to do that again. The composer was James Fulkerson, but the music was far more brassy than systems-based. And Dennis Greenwood was in it. Dennis had been one of my dancers from 1977 onwards – for twelve years, in almost everything I made, and he played a very important part as a real facilitator. Steve Paxton called him 'the star of the postmodern' in dance, because of what he contributed to the development of the aesthetic, while at the same time his name was not really widely known outside dance.

He worked with me on **Body as Site** (1992-1993) and right on up to **Unbroken View** (1994-1995), as a great contributor to my work. He was an interpreter of the work, in the sense that he had already digested the idea into his own, minimalist conceptual baggage, and that worked, up to a particular point, over one major phase of the work I was making. He was fully engaged over that period in the underground dance and film movement – if I can call it that – in London at that time. He worked with very interesting people, and he wasn't interested in being a technical dancer, although he did have a very particular technique – he was very tall and slim, with very long hair in the seventies manner, very thoughtful, intelligent and idiosyncratic. But the dance press didn't warm to him in the late 1980s and early 1990s – so that if *I* wasn't 'the problem', for the dance press, then he was. In **Body as Site** the instruction to the dancers was simply to take three places in the body, and he was so economical, with his sense of self. But he was working with a play of surfaces, and that wasn't what I then moved on to look at. In all of the period when I worked with him, there was, if you like, the absence of a focus on the dancer as person and instead the focus was on system, or construct, or grid, on lines drawn.

Then there was a definite shift for me personally [in terms of a death in the family], and in a sense there was an attempt to retrieve something personal from layers which were not on the surface. The linear sequence in **d1**, **d2**, **3D** (1989-1990) was a reaction to **After the Crying and the Shouting** (1989), which was itself a major philosophical shift, but I didn't start to do anything with that until **Unbroken View** (1994-1995), and in the installation piece, **After the Last Sky** (1995), and **Fractured Landscapes** (1995-1997).

After the Last Sky (from Edward Said's *After the Last Sky: Palestinian Lives*, with Jean Mohr, photographer, Random House, 1986) was about family, place, identity and loss. I tended in general to pick things up which I seemed to recognise, and the book was quite prominent in political and cultural section of bookshops. In general I don't really look back at the recorded past, in terms of published histories, although in this case the book was in some sense a photographic history of loss. There is some quality that photographic portraits can grasp, which interests me. All of these decisions, at that time, were in the direction of making a piece that wasn't about live performance. I was actually trying to confound the surface, the systems and grids and machines. At that time, I thought that I'd not miss the live performance, but I did. It isn't quite the same now [in 2004 and 2005], but then I did miss it.

The inspiration was a video piece, by Gary Hill, and came from walking along a corridor called *Tall Ships* (Gary Hill, 1992, a twelve-channel video installation), where there was an interaction between the live and the video. I realised suddenly that it was possible to engage with the live and with video, and with performance that is not live. So there was a technological shift starting which runs through right up to the present [in 2005]. We went up to the Museum of Modern Art in Oxford, to see this installation. I wasn't interested in the interactive, but I found that I could be moved by going down a dark corridor and turning to see a surface that was revealed because I stepped on something at floor level. Someone was revealed, with arms folded, and gradually walked towards where I was standing, and then away. And gradually as you walked down the corridor, in this gallery installation, then of course there were different dimensions of revealing, and it was haunting.

That made me feel that there could be a sense of being present, with a tall, life-sized human figure, as in **After the Last Sky**, and you could engage in dance terms with a sense of where this person was, because at this stage, they were still dancers, and they were still dancing [whereas more recent work is upper torso limited, effectively video portraiture].

One of my instructions to the dancers was 'mundane activities'. Jonathan Burrows did up his belt, and Dennis Greenwood – who was very minimalist at this stage – did and undid his shoelaces! The film

1992-95
Royal College of Art;
Gulbenkian Gallery; Ferens
Gallery, Hull; New Moves,
Glasgow; Angel Row,
Nottingham; Guildford
Cathedral; and film:
Arts Council of England,
Taped Awards

1997
The Royal College of Art

1999
Dance Festival, Dublin;
Hayward Gallery, London;
Kalamata Festival, Greece;
Dance Festivals: Ghent,
Lucerne, Rio

1995-97
Royal College of Art,
London; Gulbenkian
Gallery, London

2000-2001
Danz on Camera Festival, Oslo;
Dance on Film, The Place,
London; and touring
internationally

was wonderful. I need to film it again, on DVD this time. The Arts Council in Jerusalem wanted the piece, but there was no money to take it there. It would be very poignant now [in August 2005, after Said's death and the withdrawal of settlers from Gaza].

Then there was a twenty-year retrospective of my work at the Royal College of Art, London. There was to be a collaboration with Brian Eno, which didn't come together. Then there was a retrospective of the gallery work, specifically – none of the big dance pieces. I have all of the material, but there was no money at the time for editing it. There needs to be an archive which interweaves documented material from the originals, and then the up-to-date reworking. I had a research award from the Arts Council of England, but the processes are so expensive.

Scan (1999) comes next. And this is already much written about in essays included here. Vong Phaophanit was of great importance to me. He had been a Turner [Prize] short-listed candidate, around 1994, and he was very widely known at the time. He had a piece called 'Neon Rice Fields', which I greatly liked. He was also a Public Artist [making work in public, civic spaces], which was important. A number of artists at that time were working with the environment, and negotiating their work [rather than confronting institutions as had 'radicalised' artists earlier in the twentieth century]. The person who supported that sort of work was the curator Greg Hilty, who was at the Riverside when I was there, and who used to be at the Hayward Gallery and is now head of London Arts. Vong helped me make **Scan** – he said it reminded him of a boxing ring, and he added a film, of the piece going backwards, projected onto the floor. The piece finished, after nineteen minutes, and he had produced an abstract version of me making it, going right back to the studio work, and including images of work in the studio, and he projected the film onto the floor.

For me the whole piece was about an attempt to take on a concept of looking at the inside of the body from the outside. So there was the idea of reading an X-ray; and all of the material came from the idea of rebuilding a body, through the joints and the bones. The sense was there that it was a photographic negative as opposed to a positive, which in fact is impossible with a live body.

The dancers didn't know anything about what I was actually looking at. They were given very particular things to achieve, in the sense of their own understanding of small fragments, and I pieced a lot of material together like a jigsaw – the parts that related to what I was thinking. The dancers basically aimed to achieve a series of small results. They had no sense of the design elements, although they always had a sense that things would be half-lit, and that they would disappear into the darkness and then come out of it. It was a rhythm of juxtaposition of light and dark, seeing and non-seeing – a long-held obsession of mine, because you can't wipe away anything in dance once you've made it. You can remove it, but you can't unmake it once it's in front of you.

I realised in **Scan** that I was on the edge of a research idea but if I'd gone down that path the piece wouldn't have been made, so there's a compromise. But the thesis is produced in a sense in the making of the work – but it's different as well because in this case the 'thesis' depends on how I can use the particular skills of the professional dancer. When I look at the images, in **Scan**, there was a devised physicality that I would not now want to work with. I realised looking back that the piece was still dominated by the skills of the professional dancer, and I hadn't yet – I was trying to decrease those skills while using them. **Scan** was odd in a sense because instead of everything happening in a linear manner, it all happened at once, so there was a great density, and people in it are almost on top of each other. So the material emerged as a linear sequence, but then I squashed it together, and I evaded the dance-conventional progression. The mass of conflict came from that piling up of bodies.

I made **Images Every Three Seconds** (2003) just before **White** came out, almost as a way of getting my creative energy together while I had the three dancers with me for **White** (2003). **White** was funded by Walter Heun and his company Joint Adventures in Munich, as part of a triptych. **Images...** actually represents for me the beginning of finding the new language, through one dancer – Elena [Giannotti], in fact. I have to admit that I could not have moved forward as an artist without what she brings, which is her inner complexity. I could never have given another dancer that responsibility, to stand alone as the centre of the work, first because other dancers tended not to grasp the complexity of what I was looking for, and second because they did not have her extraordinary degree of concentration – to be able to research the idea in her own terms, but also have a photographic memory, allowing her to come up with a personal reinterpretation that she then remembers. And this process she engages in gives me the basis of what I want to see in film – almost no story, almost no dance, but then this enquiry into interiority. It is a kind of portraiture, holding back from narratives. I want to show someone experiencing something, without predetermining what that something is. She digs very deep.

In **The Hour** (2004-2005), we used a Joseph Beuys exhibition as an example – sometimes it doesn't matter what the focus of the looking is, but in his case the conceptual is so strong, informing what he makes. We were looking at a cabinet full of objects that he had put together – seven objects. I asked her to look at this collection, and then to remember a view of leaving or arriving into a room – and then in a sense the material construct plus the action will be a realisation of the abstract. The first time she attempts that sort of improvisation, because in stylistic terms she has a real ballet technique, there is a lot of conventional material which emerges, and I have to work out how to change what she is doing while retaining what she is thinking about. That is where my work begins to inhabit hers. I enable her to leave the conventional material – and she is very excited by that process, and by its complexities. It has enabled her to understand what she is as a performer, and what dance means to her.

So, **The Hour** started off as something conventional. In terms of navigation, it tries to look at the inevitable result of something, rather than the whole thing. It captures the impact of something – the culmination of the effect of something on something else. The movements are unfinished – it's looking at moments in between the moments normally recorded. In a sense it is the right completion for what is normally missing. It takes the idea of an hour, and fitting it into ten minutes – which then represents a life. The triptych (which Walter Heun has enabled) actually finally consists of **Every Three Seconds**, **The Hour**, and **Hidden Voices**.

Was it Bill Viola who said [*Reasons for Knocking at an Empty House: Writings 1973-1994*, eds. B. Viola and R. Violette, MIT Press, 1995] that it is nice to arrive at a certain age, when you can cut down your own pre-empting of process. I took that on board, with **Images Every Three Seconds** (2003), and I applied an immediacy to the discovery of the material, which I've never done before and never since. It has the fleeting immediacy of discovery. It's quite two-dimensional in one way. I didn't work anything choreographic out in advance. It was made by my throwing images at Elena so she could give

2003
Tanzquartier, Vienna;
The Place, London

2004
The Place, London

something back to me very quickly. She looked at images, and responded immediately. It was performed at the Laban Centre – I was meant to be doing a more conventional piece – and it caused a stir among colleagues at the Centre, who have never mentioned the piece to me – maybe because they didn't see it as choreography. **Vanishing Point** (2004) was film, again with Elena, following the notion of the journey as a life, travelling through – I wanted to go to the desert, to film that piece, and we shot nine hours of film, which remains with the film-maker. (I'm only beginning now to grasp something of the negative implications of what can be done with digital film-making and processing.)

Hidden Voices was strange in terms of commissioning – for The Place Prize. They started by asking for five minutes of video – which I understood to be like a scrapbook. I was short-listed, and forty of us had to present something live. I presented some fragments, which John Ashford at The Place called a series of *haiku*. I got into the last twenty. I wanted to make a film, but with [the lighting designer] Charlie Balfour. I had a series of haikus but only one worked, the last one. The piece had to last fifteen minutes. I told Elena that it had to be an internal journey. She perfectly understood. When she did it the first time, she said – with a sense of irony – 'That was the whole of my life'. She performed it for ten nights in a row, at The Place, and she was devastated, and had to take a break for ten months. It wasn't actually made to win a competition. It was a haiku.

If I try now to reflect on the way I work, then it seems to me that I don't systematically order projects in advance – in the terms of recurring patterns in the way I work, but I suppose that there is a way of seeing things [in John Berger's sense of the term, *Ways of Seeing*, Penguin, 1972], which someone looking from the outside might identify. And it is the case that there is some sort of recognition between myself and the dancers I work with at present. There has to be a sympathy there. With the dancers I've worked with recently, there does have to be a sense that they are searching for something. For **Images Every Three Seconds** (2003), **White** (2003), **Hidden Voices** (2004), **Vanishing Point** (2004), and **The Hour** (2004-5), all with Elena Giannotti, what's important as a starting point is that she is on her own pedagogical journey, without necessarily going to college. In **The Return** (DVD, unpublished work in progress, 2005), Eun-Hi Kim is a postgraduate student with a trained dance background. Elena always has said that her reason for going anywhere to work with someone has been on the basis of studying with that choreographer. She wants to pick up the means to some kind of exploration, and she then goes off to explore that in her own terms.

I think that I probably spend up to three hours a week with titles, in bookshops – especially titles of biographies or fiction where there is a sense of an exploration. There aren't many writers whom I find sympathetic in those terms, so often I end up in the Philosophy section - with writers who give that sort of broader sense of searching for something. So there's a lot of research in my work, but it's not in the sense of going to the British Library. There's a very good bookshop connected to the Serpentine Gallery, which deals a lot with what is effectively topography – the strange idea that you can make a film, through a book; where you apply one medium in order to be able to go to another medium. There's a wonderful instance of a book on Berlin, writing about the city as though it were a film. I go back to certain writers.

There's a John Berger text about photocopying which involves the idea that you can replicate an idea by photocopying it, but the actual degree and intensity of the photocopier deteriorates or gets bigger; so if you transfer that idea to the making of new [dance] work, then you can actually build up the idea of a series of paper, where the images in a way brush between being faded and not faded. But a book has to be written in a certain way so that I can go off on [that sort of associative reverie]. Another writer is Paul Virilio – *The Open Sky* [Verso Books, 1997], but also the one where he deals with the visual arts exhibition in Paris – about disaster and accident [*Ce Qui Arrive*, Fondation Cartier, Paris 2002].

I found it very interesting in visual terms but also in terms of his analysis, taking the aeroplane apart and laying the burnt parts out and labelling them very precisely. I felt that this meant that perhaps you could deal with death *through that…* without dealing with death [as such]. So the labelling and the use of sources, in terms of what is probably going on in the back of my mind, is that the context constructed then enables someone else – it is distributed to someone else precisely because it isn't personal. I don't say, 'Get into my life', but I do establish some kind of framework, that other people can enter. But they enter with their own acute awareness, with regard to that sort of thing.

So I used that same sort of procedure with Elena Giannotti and then with Liz and Jenny Roche, for the most recent work, **Six Frames: Memories of Two Women** (2005), in August at Project Upstairs art space in Dublin. Looking and identifying within memory, and then physicalising the memory, and then going back into the idea again. In **Six Frames…** I started with a photo from *The Independent on Sunday* of two women in the Beslan tragedy, looking at… The question began to fascinate me: how would two sisters remember their childhood? I started by showing them a film from Beslan, from a journalist's point of view.

They then transferred that idea of looking at things that happened, that affected them, in their own lives, and each made a notated script, independently of each other, with drawings or a word or two. We went together to the Jasper Johns exhibition, in Dublin, at the Museum of Modern Art. He was showing autobiographical work, and there were thirteen frames. The two dancers are both highly analytical, one in philosophical terms, and one in strategic terms. They had no problem researching their own memories, as material to bring to the making process. They then made a score each, of thirteen pictures, from which we extracted seven frames, of seven minutes each – forty-nine minutes.

I timed them, and filmed them. They had to read what they had written as notation, not as a memory. They could move their arms, and faces, but I filmed only the upper torso. I can't deal with legs at all at the moment. But it is still quite clear that these are highly trained dancers – from the ability to focus and to intensify minute detail, that I can film. I keep it choreographic, without using a dance vocabulary of any sort. You are very stuck, as a dancer. You can fall, or walk. Their faces were what I choreographed, over the two weeks – and it couldn't be gestural.

It had to be as though they were seeing, through the notation, something with which they connected in their childhood. It is like an impulse score that each had produced, and the performance is never the same, from one day to the next, but where it comes from is the same. I added in, to their memory and their understanding, things that might give it some tempo – they had to state something, and then counteract it, which would give something… and then *something else*. In other words, the structure that I laid upon what they already had, allowed it to be once more removed, slightly, from what had been a personal memory. Working with film allows me to focus in on something. For example, I can select the focus to some extent of what the audience looks at, but with **Six Frames**, when I look at the rushes, I also know that I am not aware of what they are looking at. There is an element of endurance to it, just short

of pain; and I wanted it to be almost fifty minutes to underline that sense that something *goes on…* and that perhaps an onlooker wants it to stop, because that is a very hard thing to look at or face up to, if nothing then happens. But I find it calming – I'm not frightened by it. What they are looking at is actually irrelevant, because there is no reaction shown. So they are actually *not* expressive.

With **Hidden Voices**, with Elena Giannotti live, at The Place (2004), and then in Munich (2005), I kept it just on the edge of what I would do with film, without making film – although it is interesting to me that Tate Modern, through Dance Umbrella, is more interested in this live piece as a collision with film, than they are with film itself. They see film as something much more familiar. Film is a controlled point of view, in contrast with dance work, and the information which it carries is no longer dance-focused, or mediated in the same way by a live dancer. It becomes sculpture, I suppose – but in my work there has to be a technically-trained dancer for the film to be made. In Dublin the film records flickering detail – it is as if they are talking to their memory, not outwards to someone else, and it's important that the score was their own, and I didn't have access to it. When I went to show the work to the Tate Modern, two Visual Arts specialists were present. They said that what they found was different about the films – from, say, the work of Bill Viola, who has been very influential for me – was that the structure in what they were seeing was itself real-time-based, so that it was clear that these dancers weren't just being filmed, performing a pre-established choreographic script. It was the performers' actual composition, unfolding in time, before the onlooker, even though the film that came out of it has my signature – and it seems that I am still a choreographer!

2005
Munich

2005
Project Upstairs,
Dublin

October 2005
Tate Modern, London

Rosemary Butcher
in conversation with Susan Melrose, September 2005

TOUCH AND GO
Studio rehearsal, London 1978

ANCHOR RELAY
Riverside Studios, London 1977

ROSEMARY BUTCHER
FULL CREATIVE CV

STUDY

1965-68 Dartington College of Arts, Dance and Theatre Course (First contemporary dance student on course)

1967 Elm Grant scholarship to study at Maryland University, USA

1968 Study at The Martha Graham School, New York (Offered school scholarship)

1970-71 Study with Merce Cunningham, Trisha Brown, Yvonne Rainer, Lucinda Childs and Meredith Monk
Performed and toured with the Elaine Summers Dance Foundation

AWARDS

2003-06 AHRC Postdoctoral Fellowship in the Creative and Performing Arts, University of Surrey/Middlesex University

2002 Jerwood Award

2000 Honorary PhD, City University, London

2000-02 Fellowship, Arts Council of England

1999 Wingate Scholarship

1996-97 Visiting Fellow, Royal College of Art

1987 *Time Out* Dance and Performance Award for outstanding creative achievement

1986 GLAA award for Service to British New Dance

1977 Royal Society of Arts, travelling scholarship

WORKS

2005 **THE RETURN**

SIX FRAMES – MEMORIES OF TWO WOMEN
Liz Roche and Jenny Roche, Dublin

2004 **VANISHING POINT** (Film)
Film-maker: Martin Otter
Dancer: Elena Giannotti

HIDDEN VOICES
Lighting Concept: Charles Balfour
Dancers: Elena Giannotti, Anis Smith, Anna Holter

2003 **WHITE**
Film-maker: Martin Otter
Composer: Cathy Lane
Dancer: Elena Giannotti

IMAGES EVERY THREE SECONDS
Lighting Concept: Charles Balfour
Dancer: Elena Giannotti

2002 **STILL-SLOW-DIVIDED**
Lighting Concept: Anthony Bowne
Composer: Cathy Lane
Dancers: Rahel Vonmoos, Henry Montes, Paul Clayden, Deborah Jones

Selected performances:
Tanzquartier, Vienna
The Place, London

Selected teaching:
Mentoring, Dance Umbrella, Dublin
University College of Dance, Stockholm
Workshops, Bern, Switzerland

2000-01 **UNDERCURRENT** (Film)
Film-maker: Cathy Greenhalgh
Composer: Cathy Lane

Selected performances:
Danz on Camera Festival, Oslo, Finland
Dance on Film, The Place, London
Toured internationally

Selected teaching:
University of Limerick, Ireland
Joint Adventures Festival, Munich
Dance Space, Edinburgh

1999 -2000 **SCAN**
Visual artist: Vong Phaophanit
Composer: Cathy Lane
Dancers: Henry Montes, Lauren Potter, Fin Walker, Jonathan Burrows

Selected performances:
Dance Festival, Dublin
Hayward Gallery, South Bank Centre, London
Kalamata Festival, Greece
Dance Festival, Ghent
Dance Festival, Lucerne
Dance Festival, Rio

Selected teaching:
Tanzstadt, Munich, Germany
Workshops, Bern, Switzerland

1998 **RESEARCH AWARD**
Arts Council of England

1997 **IN RETROSPECT** (Retrospective)

Performance:
Royal College of Art,
Gulbenkian Gallery, London

1995-97 **FRACTURED LANDSCAPES, FRAGMENTED NARRATIVES**
Visual Artist: Noel Bramley
Composer: Jonny Clark
Dancers: Henry Montes, Fin Walker

Selected performances:
RCA, Gulbenkian Gallery, (In progress performance) Feb 1977
Dance Umbrella, Autumn 1997
Arken Gallery, Copenhagen, Denmark
New Moves, Glasgow, UK

Selected teaching:
Mentoring - Scottish Choreographers, Scottish Dance Production Agency
Mentoring - Choreographers, South East Dance Agency

1995 **AFTER THE LAST SKY** (Installation)
Film-maker: David Jackson
Composer:Simon Fisher-Turner
Dancers: Dennis Greenwood, Russell Maliphant, Jonathan Burrows, Fin Walker, Deborah Jones, Gill Clarke

Selected performances:
RCA, Gulbenkian Gallery, London

UNBROKEN VIEW
Visual Artist: Sigune Hamann
Composer: Simon Fisher-Turner
Dancers: Fin Walker, Dennis Greenwood, Desiree Kongerod

Selected performances:
RCA, Gulbenkian Gallery, London
South Hill Park Gallery, Bracknell
Version: '**Unbroken View Extended Frame**'; made for Group N, in Scotland; performed at the Tramway Theatre, Glasgow

1992-93 **BODY AS SITE**
(Barclay's New Stages Award)
Artists: Paul Eliman, Ron Haselden, John Lyall, Anya Gallacio
Composer: Simon Fisher-Turner
Dancers: Deborah Jones, Fin Walker, Gill Clarke, Dennis Greenwood, Michael Popper, Michelle Smith

Selected performances:
RCA, Gulbenkian Gallery, London
Ferens Gallery, Hull
New Moves, Glasgow
Angel Row Gallery, Nottingham
Guildford Cathedral
Film: Body as Site, Arts Council of England, Taped Awards

1991 **OF SHADOWS AND WALLS**
Film-maker: Nicola Baldwin
Music: James Fulkerson
Dancers: Fin Walker, Michael Popper, Angela Brown,

Selected performances:
Riverside Studios, London
The Royal Festival Hall, London

1989-90 **d1, d2, 3D**
Architect (d1): Zaha Hadid
Architect (d2, 3D): John Lyall
Composer: James Fulkerson
Dancers: Lauren Potter, Dennis Greenwood, Catherine, Fin Walker,

Selected performances:
Royal Festival Hall, d1
Spitalfields Church, d2
Tramway Theatre Glasgow, 3D

UK National Tour with teaching workshops

Selected teaching:
National University workshops

1989   **SILENT SPRING**

AFTER THE CRYING AND THE SHOUTING
Visual Artist: Ron Haselden
Composer: Wim Mertens
Dancers: Gary Rowe, Fin Walker,
Dennis Greenwood, Caroline Allen,
Lyn Denton, Wendy Thomas

Selected performances:
ICA London
BBC2, The Late Show

Selected teaching:
Summer Residency English Dance Theatre,
Newcastle

1988   **TOUCH THE EARTH**
Television, BBC 2, *Dancemakers*

1987   **TOUCH THE EARTH**
Visual Artist: Heinz Dieter Pietsch
Composer: Michael Nyman
Dancers: Jonathan Burrows,
Sue MacLennan, Dennis Greenwood,
Maedee Dupres, Helen Rowsell,
Caroline Pegg, Alex, Wendy Thomas,
Yolanda Snaith, Gary Rowe

Selected performances:
Whitechapel Art Gallery, London
QE Hall, South Bank Centre, London
British National Tour of thirty Galleries

Selected teaching:
ILEA, London Schools' performances

1986   **TEN YEARS ON 9** (Retrospective)

Selected performances:
Riverside Studios, London
UK National Tour

Selected teaching:
Schools' Educational Residency, Bristol

1986   **FLYING LINES**
Visual Artist: Peter Noble
Composer: Michael Nyman
Dancers: Jonathan Burrows,
Sue MacLennan, Dennis Greenwood,
Maedee Dupres, Helen Rowsell,
Caroline Pegg, Alex, Wendy Thomas,
Yolanda Snaith, Gary Rowe

Selected performances:
QE Hall, South Bank Centre, London
Riverside Studios, London
Bagnolet Festival, Paris
UK National Tour

1984   **NIGHT MOORING STONES**
Film-maker: Jane Rigby
Composer: Max Eastly
Dancers: Gaby Agis, Dennis Greenwood,
Helen Rowsell

Selected performances:
Riverside Studios, London

Television, Channel 4,
SPACES 4
Dancers: Gaby Agis, Helen Rowsell,
Dennis Greenwood

1983   **TRACES**
Sculptor: Heinz Dieter Pietsch
Composer: Tom Dolby
Dancers: Dennis Greenwood,
Sue MacLennan, Miranda Tufnell

Selected performances:
Riverside Studios, London
National Tour
International Dance Festival, Utrecht

IMPRINTS
Visual artist: Heinz Dieter Pietsch
Composer: Malcolm Clarke

THE SITE
Visual artist: Heinz Dieter Pietsch
Composer: Malcolm Clarke

1982   **SHELL; FORCE FIELDS AND SPACES**
Visual Artist: Jon Groom
Composer: James Fulkerson
Dancers: Julyen Hamilton,
Maedee Dupres, Beverly, Sue MacLennan

Selected performances:
ICA, London
Arnolfini Gallery, Bristol
Dance Festival, Rome

FIELD BEYOND THE MAPS
Composer: Jim Fulkerson

1981   **SPACES 4**
Sculptor: Heinz Dieter Pietsch

LANDSCAPE
Composer: George Crumb

SOLO DUO
Dancers: Sue MacLennan,
Rosemary Butcher, Dennis Greenwood,
Laurie Booth, Gaby Agis, Helen Rowsell

Selected performances:
Riverside Studios, London
National Tour

1979   **FIVE SIDED FIGURE**
Visual Artist: Jon Groom
Composer: Jane Wells
Dancers: Janet Smith, Julyen Hamilton,
Sue MacLennan, Rosemary Butcher

Selected performances:
Riverside Studios, London

SIX TRACKS

SOLO FROM INSTRUCTION

1978   **CATCH FIVE – CATCH SIX**

TOUCH AND GO

UNEVEN TIME

SUGGESTION AND ACTION

DANCES FOR DIFFERENT SPACES
Dancers: Sylvie Panet-Raymond, Emily
Barney, Sue MacLennan, Kirstie Simpson

Selected performances:
Riverside Studios, London
National Tour
International Dance Festival, Paris

1977   **SPACE BETWEEN**

WHITE FIELD
Music: Colin Wood

THEME

EMPTY SIGNALS
Music: Colin Wood

ANCHOR RELAY
Dancers: Maedee Dupres, Julyen Hamilton,
Sue MacLennan, Dennis Greenwood,
Miranda Tufnell

Selected performances:
Riverside Studios, London
Dartington Festival

1976   **Rosemary Butcher Dance Company formed**

MULTIPLE EVENT

GROUND LINE

PAUSE AND LOSS
Sound: Alan Lamb
Dancer: Brigitta Petterson

Selected performances:
Serpentine Gallery, London

LANDINGS
Sound: Alan Lamb
Dancers: Brigitta Petterson, Maedee Dupres,
Peter Page (Julyen Hamilton),
Sue MacLennan

Selected performances:
Serpentine Gallery, London

PASSAGE NORTH EAST
Dancers: Miranda Tufnell, Eva Karzag,
Maedee Dupres, Sue MacLennan,
Peter Page (Julyen Hamilton)

Selected performances:
Riverside Studios, London
Arnolfini Gallery, Bristol
Outside Spaces, City of London Festival

1974   **UNEVEN TIME**
For Scottish Theatre Ballet's Moveable
Workshop's Tour of Scotland.

BIOGRAPHIES OF AUTHORS

Robert Ayers is an English-born, Manhattan-based performance artist, who until recently was Professor of Contemporary Arts at Nottingham Trent University, UK. He is a widely published writer, teacher, and curator.

Ian Bramley is a freelance writer and arts consultant. He is the former Director of Dance UK and was the Editor of *Dance Theatre Journal* and Head of Publications at Laban, London from 1998 to 2003, where he established the academic dance journal, *Discourses in Dance*. He was the first recipient of the Chris de Marigny Dance Writers' Award in 1995.

Janet Lansdale is Distinguished Professor in Dance Studies at the University of Surrey. She has published four books on aspects of dance theory and has another due on intertextuality in dance. She has run a doctoral programme for many years from which thirty-six students have graduated. She has been a board member for the Arts and Humanities Research Council, the Society for Dance History Scholars and the Society for Dance Research.

Josephine Leask is a dance writer and lecturer. She is London correspondent for *The Dance Insider*, www.danceinsider.com, and contributes to *Ballet International* and *Dance Theatre Journal*. She lectures on Cultural Studies at the London Studio Centre.

Susan Leigh Foster is a choreographer, dancer, and writer, and is currently Professor at UCLA Department of World Arts and Cultures. She is the author of *Reading Dancing* (University of California Press, 1986), *Choreography and Narrative* (Indiana University Press, 1996) and (Wesleyan University Press, 2003). She is editor of (Indiana, 1995) and (Routledge, 1996).

Nadine Meisner is a London-based dance writer and critic. She has been deputy editor of the monthly magazine *Dance & Dancers* and a regular contributor over two decades to *The Times, The Sunday Times, The Daily Telegraph* and *The Independent*. She has viewed and reviewed Rosemary Butcher's work almost since its first appearance and has written extensively about it, in both the specialist and national press.

Susan Melrose is Professor of Performing Arts at Middlesex University. After postgraduate studies in Paris, she taught in France, Tunisia, Turkey and Australia before returning to the UK, where she established postgraduate programmes in the 1990s at the Central School of Speech and Drama, and Rose Bruford College. She is widely published in performance analysis, and a major contributor to the national debate, in the university, on the 'knowledge status' of professional arts practices. Her *Semiotics of the Dramatic Text* was published by Macmillan in 1994.

Niki Pollard is currently working towards an AHRC-funded doctorate, concerned with co-authored practitioner writing of dance making, at Middlesex University. She holds an undergraduate degree from Cambridge (Corpus Christi College) and an MA from the Laban Centre for Movement and Dance, where she was also research assistant to Rosemary Butcher.

Hugh Stoddart worked in the visual arts through the 1970s, finally as Director of the Ikon Gallery, Birmingham. He became a full-time writer following the success of his screenplays – notably *To the Lighthouse* and his original screenplay *Remembrance*. Other films from the 1980s include *We Think the World of You* with Alan Bates and Gary Oldman. In 1992, his original drama serial about religious faith and intolerance *The Big Battalions* was on Channel Four. His adaptation of *The Mill on the Floss* was shown on BBC1 in 1997 and in 2002 BBC 1 showed *Dialogues of the Dead*. He has remained in touch with the visual arts as a critic and writer of catalogue essays and contributed to a book celebrating the work of Irish artist Tony O'Malley.

Prep for PASSAGE NORTH EAST South Bank, London 1976